Reluctant Prophets

Reluctant Prophets

by J.D. Isip

MOON
TIDE PRESS

~ 2025 ~

Reluctant Prophets

Editor-in-chief
Eric Morago

Editor Emeritus
Michael Miller

Marketing/Social Media Specialist
Ellen Webre

Operations Associate
Shelly Holder

Proofreader
Mackensi E. Green

Front cover art
Solomon Joseph Solomon,
"Ajax and Cassandra" (1886)

Author photo
Amanda Migues

Book design
Michael Wada

Moon Tide logo design
Abraham Gomez

Reluctant Prophets
is published by Moon Tide Press

Moon Tide Press
6709 Washington Ave. #9297
Whittier, CA 90608
www.moontidepress.com

FIRST EDITION

Printed in the United States of America

ISBN # 978-1-957799-28-5

for my Texas family
The Ferrier-Watsons

Contents

The Prophets

The Lonely

The Leaving

The Living

The lie is that seeing the world without you
will make enduring this world easier.

—James Davis May, "Sentimental Hogwash"

Don't you dare sum me up.

—Tom from *All Over the Guy*

Now I understand, Kostya, that in our work—it doesn't matter
whether we act or we write—the main thing isn't fame, glamour,
the things I dreamed about, it's knowing how to endure.

—Nina from *The Seagull*

This life has shown me how we're mended and how we're torn
How it's okay to be lonely as long as you're free
Sometimes my ground was stony
And sometimes covered up with thorns
And only You could make it what it had to be

—Rich Mullins, "Elijah"

Foreword

Author Robert Benson tells the story of a five-year-old girl "who claims she talks to God and that God talks back." He goes on to explain that even people who believe in God will say, "It is cute of course that she thinks that, and then they will pat the child on the head as though they are certain that, in time, she will grow out of it." We all know that she will grow out of it, that life will knock her down, that she will succumb to the darkness that erases such confident wonder and hope—the darkness that "swallows us up whole, our soft and trembling bodies / cast into the dark shafts of this cracked world where we keep on falling."

In the lines and stanzas of *Reluctant Prophets*, we experience hell on earth; together, we know pain that is not our own. So, we sit down and read poems to see "what we will find down there, deep down there / on the wet unseen surfaces." In these poems and prose pieces, J.D. Isip searches the depths because he is very good at it. He's good at asking questions and sharing pain. I know, because I sat in his living room as he asked me about my story, the hours passing late into the night. We discussed the "Hard Stuff," even when we knew it would burn…"Oh God, it burns!"

Jonah, the most reluctant prophet, called out to God from the belly of the fish. He said, "You cast me into the deep, into the heart of the seas!" Jonah knew something of wet, unseen surfaces. He knew hell under the "billows and waves." In much the same way, we sit with these words, hoping for deliverance, and not believing it's possible, but reading "against oblivion" all the same. J.D. brings us "back to believing something like peace, even in the darkest of times, is a possibility." Like Jonah and the five-year-old girl, we call out in our distress, and in lines and stanzas, God talks back.

— W. Scott Cheney

Nineveh, Again

"This, too, was a great city once, a city on a hill,"
I would say to Jonah, sitting beneath the shade
of a tree that sprouted up overnight, "This place,
too, seemed to come up out of nowhere,

A miracle, at least in the retelling, certainly not
to the 31 dead pilgrims, or the Natives," I'd say,
offering him a piece of bread, "And I've waited
for the moon to fall apart, wipe the board,"

He'd smile, decline the broiled fish, "It's evil
to wish for Armageddon, I know, but leaving
it as is, indolent and self-satisfied, barely worth
a warning—let it all go down, deep down,"

And Jonah'd go quiet, looking over the Rockies,
a herd of bison with fur like sackcloth, jazz clubs
on Bourbon Street, the caged flame of Liberty,
and the dark Atlantic waters, "Maybe," he'd offer,

"Maybe we call it a night, who knows how long
this redwood or earth will be here, let us sleep
and we will either wake to Judgement Day or
another morning in America, like it or not."

The Prophets

Ionas puppe cadens, Ceto forbente voratus,
In pelago non senfit aquas, vitale sepulcrum

Ne moreretur habens, tandemqz e ventre ferino
Venit ad ignotas tutus fine remige terras.

The heart does not want to go up.
The bones whip it there, driving it
with a terrible music of the spirit.

— Linda Gregg, "The Men Like Salmon"

The Real Thing

I fashion myself a Cassandra
holding tight my premonitions
and little else. Nothing else.

Her text says *I'm in loooove!!*
my room dark but her screen, enough
exclamations and emojis to see doom

blossom on the horizon, my talent
for sight—or good ol' fashioned rain
clouding: *Again?* Nothing more.

Before the divorce, he found me,
clapped my shoulders, "This is it!"
another punctuation for the doubts

or my familiar warnings. To tell
the truth, I once thought (imagine!),
was all we ever need to do.

Nothing else. Nothing more. But
truth is a light all mortals blot out
and silence her wordy prophets.

Zest

Essential Oils Prophetess
white girl with calves like grapefruit
her pomelo ass saran wrapped in a white
pencil skirt says to smell her hand, lifts it

under your nose, pure orange zest like happiness
squeezed out in miniscule droplets, tiny,
effervescent, fleeting joy, you almost
lick her wrist, you ask how much

it's not cheap, you could buy bags of fruit
for weeks, but think of the clementines
wrinkling in the drawer of the fridge
all the fruit you've let waste away

there are oils for cooking, too, she says,
clients sometimes love this one and the lemon
so much they want to put it in everything, but
it'll make you sick, too much of it.

The Homily

Baby snakes in a mason jar, a boy thinks they are worms,
harmless food for fish he will catch with his father later
in the afternoon. This is the first clue: everybody knows
you don't go fishing that late in the day. O the innocence!

Chaplain Wang, who'd clearly never gone fishing a day
in her life, lifted the story like tiny, poison bodies, fed it
to the hungry airmen in her chapel, a misheard lesson
she would embellish with the trip to the lake, the father,

who she meant to be Christ, was waiting at the wrong time
of day, had sent his son, too young to see the serpent's body
is nothing like a worm. This was the way of this world
according to her: If your son asks for food, give a lesson.

The Lowest Part of the Ship

Send me not to that great city
Send me not with this message
It does not roll off the tongue
Nor should it

To escape one must go inward first or swallow yourself up,
grabbing each half of your mouth and pulling down like
a pair of socks, your tongue a nice handle or hook to carry
you along or hang you up, "I'm fine" or "It's nothing" or
nothing, nothing, nothing with your mouth wide open.

It does not leave light from the lips
Nor should it

Then you're reading the texts. A friend. A colleague. God.
Everyone worries you'll do it again, you'll take the car or plane
or boat, climb yourself down to the lowest part of the ship, stop
reading their texts, put your face down into a pillow, say or
scream nothing into it, dissolve, pull yourself down.

It does not come free from this man
Nor can it

When Jesus did it, when his men were shouting their own inanity,
he slept, and you only want to sleep through this current tragedy.
Is that too much to ask? To be left alone to your own devices,
maybe a drink or two, a lover or two, fire or ice or a razor, or
a last resort, "Please! Please throw me over!"

Nor should it
Nor will it

Ignorance

Shall we give pugilism another go? Go each of us
to a corner to gather ourselves, rhetorically that is
together our selves which are the better halves we
have within each of us, or thirds or fourths, a fourth
seems so miniscule a portion to measure out when
we are out here brawling it out, out of our own minds
with our ancient rage. What was it anchored in?

That nascent slight thorned into an unreachable chamber
as if by accident—and, by God, perhaps it was!—to niggle
itself into ourselves with such subtlety we wouldn't suspect
what was growing in the dark like spores in the cold black
aspect where what we expect of ourselves is better, brighter
even than what we will find down there, deep down there
on the wet unseen surfaces where it reproduces,
reproduces, reproduces, reproduces…

What We Deserve
for Matt Chandler

One of my best friends, he posts, this poet I know, *died—*
and I found out on Facebook. Fucking Facebook. This poet,
who isn't dead, tells Facebook, *he deserved more than this*,
and he means the best friend, but he also means himself.
Probably more himself. "You want answers?" Col. Jessep

is cold-eyed, snarling. There's a reason Nicholson has three
Oscars. It is *one of* the best in movie history. This scene quoted
by Pastor Matt last Sunday. Tom Cruise, "I want the truth—"
and anyone of my generation, older than we ever imagined
ourselves, can say it from heart, "You can't handle the truth!"

This is church online, church on YouTube, fucking YouTube,
"We've moved from the idea that truth is outside of me—"
I never got along with his husband, the poet confesses, truth,
"Something fixed, something set," the pastor has a statistic,
"91% of Americans believe the words, *The best way to find*

yourself is by looking within yourself." The poet is precious
in his own story. What he deserves is better than Facebook,
better than the sideline obscurity, better than being the last
to know. Colonel Jessep is not the good guy. There are so few
good men, "You have the luxury of not knowing what I know."

That *one of* paired with *best friend* doesn't make sense, though
we all say it. That spouse will trump best friend. That you are
only *one of*. That there are walls and deaths and choices, truths
too rigid and clear to accept. So, we escape somewhere within
ourselves, we all do it, believing, *I deserve better than this*.

The Hard Stuff

The smell could make your eyes hurt. You believed
it would take the varnish off the kitchen table. Nothing
could make you take a sip back then. Back when dad
would cup the snifter under your nose, "Take a drink,
son," he'd tease, watching you squirm. "A real man,"
he would say, as your brother moved you aside, "Drinks
what he's given." When my brother lost the first baby,
he didn't make a big deal. My father is dying, slowly,
but he doesn't mention it. "It burns! Oh god, it burns!"
I say about most of this life. Because it does. It does.

Kingmakers Anonymous

Samuel
History will blame me, but what do I care?
Fools simping after freedom or ideology, cry
"Give us a king," and I comply. The tallest
man among them, the one most likely to kill
more than any other man, give him a kingdom,
whatever words of wisdom you care to waste,
and, in the end, a part of yourself. Your part
in this tragic trajectory, "Saul is your king!"

Merlin
Come now! Don't tell us the magic isn't, well,
tempting. One day it's hat tricks, becoming, oh,
an owl or squirrel or some apparition, next day
it's the horn of oil or the sword in the stone, you
with the power to right the current, to rewrite him
out of destiny. What a spell! Rise, you gold spires,
you waving herald banners, you naïve boy, arrogant
wizard, king, Camelot, queen, Lancelot! Damned
close to perfection. Damn. Damn it all.

Falstaff
Can we drink to that? I'd drink to that. Damn it all!
Damn these boy kings! You want to know magic?
Take you a whisp of a man, take him to the people,
to the drunkards and whores, to the only people who
matter in this world because we are what it is really.
Teach him to woo, to steal, to play the innocent. Hal,
my boy, my all, not as sweet as I thought! He said,
to me, to *me*, he would be the sun. The bloody sun!

Obi-Wan
Hello, there! Sorry I am late, my friends. Did I miss anything? Ha! Did *I* miss anything? Didn't we all miss the signs? Not even signs, prophecies! Like smitten little girls, look at us flitting after these broken men! What do we think? There is enough will in us, enough force to forge a better future than that which was preordained? Gentlemen, no. What good has free will done for any of us? Burned down our galaxies!

Merlin: Our hopes!
Falstaff: Our hearts!
Samuel: Our hour is up. Thank God.

Slurring Your Words

How to ask what happened. Each word unfurls
at half-speed, each phrase—he left, my diagnosis,
never came back, the voices—edge at meaning.

I remember you say, voice cracking, all of it, of us
crumbles, *you and me in the tower, looking over
Florence,* it was a cold winter, we were beautiful

and I loved you then, before you married, we lost
ourselves in the arms of men, our own ambitions,
you're crying, *we went skiing in Cortina, remember?*

The alcohol, men, sex, schizophrenia, hard to say,
I love you when we have been sacked and pillaged
by our own wayward digressions, it takes such effort

with men like us, to survive what we thought endless
we ate our hearts, bit by bit, even as they froze to ice
leaving our lips numb, slurring our echoes of affection.

The Cloud of Unknowing

for Ellen Caldwell

There is beauty in the immensity of our ignorance,
like the large eyes and rounded head of an infant, knowing
nothing, admitting or accepting as much, reaching out
to the waters of the abyss, our tiny hands and tiny minds
grasping for whatever it is we hope will love us back.

"Roll your Rs like this," and you'd half-sing Chaucer,
eyes blithe, one hand gesturing the motion of words
like a carriage on some country road, hills and dales
and the original Robin Hood tales, every tree a home,
every story a hint at immortality or, at least, a bigger life.

Pete and I in the front row, the entire class leaning in,
following your quick and clipped responses, your smile
when we'd say we couldn't get the language, the jokes
were not funny, the world of Olde Englande spoke
nothing to us and our more important moment of now.

By the end of the semester, we were all in love. The Miller,
The Clerk, The Wife of Bathe, the impossibly small
woman in a Puritan style skirt, short cropped white hair,
the kind of patience that comes from suffering, from
endurance. By the end, you enlarged our tiny worlds.

There was a sister. A home in Los Angeles. What a drive.
There was mostly unknowing. Even now, it galls me
to have said I love someone and know nearly nothing
of who you were, except that when I told Pete, we
felt the universe contract, but in the good way,

the way it does before it bursts forth anew.

Billows & Waves
Jonah 2:3

"That bastard didn't want to let go," Robyn tells me about riding a whale. I'm not sure where the struggle takes place, what body of water he's talking about. His stories start in Fiji but always end up somewhere else—Mai Khao in Phuket, or a boarding school outside Melbourne, or a flight to the States.

Sandy, in the kitchen, hands me a mug of tea for her husband and says, "Don't believe everything he tells you, but that story" the one about the whale, "that one is true." They met on that flight. He played rugby. She served drinks to him and a dozen other players, living off their good looks, a little charm, promise.

I ask Robyn about his surgery, the third in two years. He smiles, "There's this big goddamn robot thing," this is also true, "and I asked the doctor if I could come and see it," he starts scrolling through pictures on his phone, their granddaughter on a horse, his sister in a wheelchair, an old black and white, "Look at this!"

It's Robyn, maybe 18 or 19, shirtless skinny body, that 70s hair, he's holding these enormous fish by their jaws, one in each hand, he's smiling like he's in a beer commercial. I picture Sandy, a navy blue number with white hemming, laughing at the boys in first-class (on someone else's dime) trying to get her number. "The whale?"

Sean, their son, guesses the story I'm interested in, "I tell my dad maybe he shouldn't tell it anymore, people will get mad you killed a whale, even if it was a long time ago." He's right, of course. People never let you finish the story. Which is why you have to keep trying to tell it the right way before all the billows and waves take over.

Reluctant Prophet

Pour myself a cup of… a vision.

I actually asked her, "How will I feed my dogs?" It was a good year until it wasn't. There's always the ones "just following orders," and those with the temerity to point it out. I saw fire, as foretold, fell the false prophets. Convinced myself I had something to do with it, but I am only an instrument. I offer myself, empty and echoing all the truths that make you stop up your ear, quicken your step, wonder why my ilk are always so filthy.

Folks like me, on the job…

My life could have been worse, cooking my meals on feces or giving my heart to a whore who, as foretold, would give it away in pieces to anyone looking for a nibble. Everyone will praise your bravery while backing into the shrubbery. Giving myself to a 9-to-5 knowing full-well what Prophet Dolly told me. Sometimes you don't need the gift, just your eyes and history.

What a way to… make an enemy.

History says hold out for the chariots. Cold comfort when packing up a life. Because I tell you, there is always a Jezebel or an Ahab, or a vice/associate/middle manager, "just doing her job," who sends you an email after your most glorious victory. They are not unique; they multiply like maggots. "I will not rest," she says, tossing slabs of raw flesh at her hounds, "I will see you die."

Barely getting by…

They usually do, too. She enjoyed seeing my weakness, could almost taste the blood. When the walls are breached, the city sacked, the prophets who saw it all coming are often the first to the fire. It's fitting, we were made for sacrifice. I just thought it would be more glorious. I'd give a speech. People would weep. Every character in this play sees themselves the martyr.

It's all taking and no… glory.

Instead, you run to the nearest wasteland, someplace to be more
alone than the alone you've always known. You want to die, or
to stop caring. You try not answering the phone, not showering
a day or two, a week even. Go without food. But hope is as cruel
as life itself, sending ravens with bits of bread, honey in a carcass,
kindnesses, even a new job, a second wind, and more to say when
you wanted silence.

It's enough to drive you… if you let it.

It is always profitable until it isn't. Puttin' money in your pockets.
Then gallows and guillotines, bullets with your name on them.
Delay. Deny. Defend. Because I tell you, the dogs *will* be fed.

Jehovah Shammah

Was it you, O Lord, who lifted this lifeless self
      to breathe-in your world
      to tremble before wind and icy days
      to drink and to drink too much
      to remember and to cry,
And did You know the clay would come to this
            in a bar somewhere, alone?

Was it You, my God, who called to black velvet shapes
      to cradle heaven and her constellations
         who called to burning mountains
      to release shadow-black birds like arrows aimed at the sun
         who called to the beasts of the field
      to bow before these lower, less noble forms
         who take their fill and scurry away…
And did You think the clay might come to this
           on a street somewhere, alone?

Was it You, O Creator, who shaped man's soul
      to hunger for self and to thirst for sin
         who placed on men eyes
      to long for flesh and to worship it
         who gave man a will
      to be constant as rain, loyal as Luck
         who put in men minds
      to crack and spill and hold nothing…
And could You guess the clay would be this
           in a bed somewhere, alone?

Was it You, O Lord, who came to this lifeless place
      to breathe-in Yourself
      to tremble before doubt and icy faith
      to love and to love too much
      to remember and to cry?
Yet, You knew the clay would come to this
           in a garden somewhere, alone.

Tiles & Floods

Here is a story for the next time you are looking up at a tiled ceiling. These things are a relic of the 70s and 80s, mostly you see them in hospitals and some schools. Every time I've seen them, they have water damage. I don't know what that is about. Seems to me there's something in it about catastrophe. How floods and cracked pipes and tears are only ever a day away. If you're in Vegas, you might still see these in the really old hotels. If you're in one of those, you're not in Vegas for fun. So, when you see these, you're in something old and you're probably bored. We used to knock out single tiles and hide things in the empty space above— nothing consequential, nothing like a time capsule (at least not an intentional one).

I used to get paid to tell the story of Walt Disney. I'd walk folks around Disneyland in California and, for a little over two hours, I'd tell them all about Walt. I felt like a pastor walking around a forest or a garden and talking to believers about God. These folks were true believers. Everything I said was a wonder or a reassurance. I cost a cool $100 on top of whatever they spent to get into the park that day; there was incentive to believe. It helps that I was one of them.

I couldn't put an exact moment on my love affair with everything Disney, but I know that it never really ended. Sure, I grew up and got jaded. I took maybe one too many theory classes, read too much Baudrillard (which is to say, *any* Baudrillard). Yet, in the end, I'll still watch one of the old movies when I'm down, and I still go to visit friends at the parks whenever I am in town. I understand my tour guests, their longing for magic. I took a few classes on Irish literature and read about Yeats' longing for fairies and women and something more meaningful.

When Walt was dying of lung cancer in 1966, they hid it from the news. They explained away his hospital stay as an old hockey injury. Later, for almost forty years, the Walt Disney Company erased any remnant of a cigarette in pictures of Walt, even private ones with his family. But it *was* the cigarettes that took him down. This emblem of the American Dream was brought low by another one, and people are still arguing over whether or not cartoons are just as bad. People can be simple. People can be vicious. People can let themselves believe many things.

They say his brother, Roy, would come in to see his little brother. He'd rub his feet. As a guy with four brothers, I think this is one of many embellishments; even if they were looking at death, I'd never rub my brothers' feet. Walt was planning EPCOT, his Experimental Prototype Community of Tomorrow. This was, frankly, some dystopian bullshit with a panopticon built right in the center of the thing. Walt was definitely a futurist, but one without a filter, one who never really saw the danger in anything he dreamt up. Yes, he hired full-on Nazis to help him plan his first Tomorrowland. He wasn't a terrible person, mind you. But he wasn't a saint.

His brother, Roy, on the other hand? I'd give the Pope my vote for his sainthood. He reminds me of my siblings. A selfless guy, never looking for a spotlight. He *did* go to see his brother, who time and again put Roy's entire family in financial jeopardy, who spent years not talking to Roy because he dared to disagree with Walt; and there was Roy, at his bedside. And Walt would point to the tiles above him.

They say he was mapping out where everything was going to go in EPCOT. How the tiles to the north of his torso would surround a world showcase packed with pavilions of food and entertainment from everywhere they'd ever traveled together. He'd point to the tile above his oxygen tank and say this will be where we put the live animals I wanted in Adventureland. Do you remember those, Roy? And Roy would nod his head and wonder how many more days or even hours he had with his little brother.

My tour guests would get a little weepy toward the end. I'd recite the speech Eric Sevareid gave on CBS the night Walt died, "He was an original. Not just an American original, but an original period," and I would tell them to think about his brother Roy, who stepped out of retirement to help build Walt Disney World and, yes, pave the way for EPCOT. I said his brother was listening to this speech, "He probably did more to heal or at least sooth troubled human spirits than all the psychiatrists"—it's no wonder Foucault, Baudrillard, and the lot of them were never fans—"what Walt seemed to know was that while there is very little grown-up in a child, there is a lot of child in every grown-up"—don't suppose Freud would be a fan, either.

When I got to my doctorate program, one of the first professors I met was Susan. She was brilliant. And, like so many academics, she was well aware. I was sitting in this old as sin library-cum-conference room in the Hall of Languages, and I was staring up at the ceiling. I was nervous, of course. I was not academic enough back then to feel like a genius. Susan sat down at the table across from me and asked me who I was and why I was there. I guess I wanted to seem, I don't know, fun or informed or just say something memorable.

I said, pointing at the browned water stains on the tiled ceiling, these things always make me think of Walt Disney. She didn't look up, but said, Walt Disney was a bastard. And a racist. And I think he was antisemitic, too. I hope you don't plan on writing about Walt Disney, because you're wasting your time. Nobody cares about him anymore.

Before she retired, she was doing research on obscure dime novels. Even then I could see there was a person who once believed in magic, who once could laugh out loud. I saw her ride her horse off campus, and she looked transported. She became a kind of friend and mentor, and I told her when I graduated, I am so happy to know you. I love you. And then she just vanished. I'd hear from friends of friends how much life hit her, sick parents, dead parents, loneliness. And worse, a bitterness that comes from feeling like you've been cheated.

There's a statue of Roy Disney at Walt Disney World, but most people just assume it's Walt or they don't care at all. Most people have no idea that this American Dream was built by *two* brothers, not just the dreamer in front of the camera. Toiling in the background, cooking the books, leveraging every one of his own dreams and relationships, there was this brother. Maybe he didn't rub Walt's feet, but he saw a brother who was more than whatever these pop-culture scholars would call him. He was real, and his dreams were, too.

And some of us would rather spend our time building a goddamn ark to nowhere than every minute dreading the inevitable flood.

Don't Tell Me

for Brandon Barnes

Nothing you'll find more orphan than the heart.

— Anders Carlson-Wee, "Lodestar"

"Everyone tells me you are a fake, but I believe in you."

That the Great Pumpkin is a meditation on faith may not be news. That Linus and Lucy and Charlie Brown are all always telling us something about ourselves may also be old hat. Still. Here at the makeshift pumpkin patch at the Dallas Arboretum, by myself as usual, I hear Linus writing out his letter to the Great Pumpkin, continually interrupted by friend after friend telling him he's crazy.

There's no such thing as the Great Pumpkin. You might as well believe in Santa Claus or Superman. You might as well believe in falling in love. Or even finding love when you're this close to 50. You might as well believe in peace in the Middle East. Or Jesus. It's crazy what people will believe.

"P.S. If you really are a fake, don't tell me. I don't want to know."

Brandon holds that Linus, fool in the pumpkin patch, is a "criticism of apocalyptic preachers." It's hard to argue with Brandon. Like so many of my friends here in Texas, there's a different kind of wariness of religion. Whereas Californians are, so far as I can tell, turned off by religion in the usual ways – met too many hypocrites, maybe we tried it out and became hypocrites ourselves – the Texans I've met were almost all "religious from the start." Their skepticism, even cynicism springing from an inescapable indoctrination. So many of my friends here don't even talk to their families anymore. Or they do, but it's always guarded.

Charlie Brown comes waiving a letter in the air, "I got an invitation to a Halloween party!" He proceeds to do a little dance.

It's easy to sit back and tell folks, "I told you so." A friend who thinks she can change her boyfriend. Another who thinks she can make her kids choose a different path; she just has to try a different angle of influence. Everyone I know is waiving some sort of hope in the air, running straight for people like me to verify that what they are holding is, in fact, real.

"Charlie Brown," Lucy says, "If you got an invitation, it was a mistake."

Who knew Lucy was a Pharisee? That old Groucho Marx chestnut, "I don't want to belong to any club that will accept me as a member," makes its round in the atheism circuit. In the old days, it was a disdain for the harlots and tax collectors, then generally the sinners, but then people got real honest. They thought of their fucked-up parents or high school bullies, celebrities they hated who "found Jesus," and, of course, the ick-factor of being offered salvation themselves... knowing exactly how absurdly fucked-up *they were* – who would want to be a part of that?

"Each year, the Great Pumpkin rises out of the pumpkin patch that he thinks is the most sincere."

Linus can't help himself. Like Paul, he must add "works" to his faith. It's a clever way out, too. If you are in an insincere pumpkin patch, the problem is not the Great Pumpkin, but you and your lousy choice of waiting places. Or maybe the lack of sincerity is in the one waiting. I understand Brandon's take on the apocalyptic preachers – how can one begin to argue with a faith based on a paradox? If the Great Pumkin never shows up, there's always – *always* – the possibility the error is in the translation. It's why people will wait millennia for a promised return. Why some even hold out *after* the cheating, the abuse, the addiction, after all the wreckage.

Lucy sets her alarm to get dressed and bring her brother home from the pumpkin patch.

My favorite scene in *It's the Great Pumpkin, Charlie Brown* is when Lucy, stone-cold as she is, gets up at 4 in the morning to get her little brother and put him to bed. He's shivering under his trusty blanket. There are no words exchanged. She gets him up and walks him home. Even though she has her usual frown on, she lovingly takes off his shoes before Linus falls back into his bed. She pulls the covers over him and walks out. I told Brandon I think this is the real message – not that we are *supposed to* be believers or, as he would argue, we are *supposed to* be skeptics, but that whatever our faith-based proclivity, it should engender in others something good.

I argue Lucy is never a better person in all of *Peanuts* than in this scene.

It's fall 2023. The world is once again at war. I admit, I am a bit numb to it. With Russia and Ukraine, there seemed to be clear good guys and bad guys. Now, as with so many previous generations, it is Israel and Palestine. The lines do not seem so clear. Honestly, writers can sometimes be the worst – with our platitudes and equivocations. We can't help ourselves. We *know* the answers, of course. If only people would listen to us. What *is* our answer anyway? That *this time* we just have to make sure our peace accords are "more sincere"? I hate to sound so cynical. I'm supposed to be a person of faith, after all. But I gotta say, I am terrible at it. Sure, I'm a Jesus Freak.

"Everyone tells me you are fake, but I believe in you."

This world is all about perspective. The loneliest thing in this world is to have a perspective and find nobody who shares it. It will cause you to doubt. You might even try to see it all differently. You'll try. But sooner or later, you'll be back in that pumpkin patch. You'll be back on that dating app. You'll be back in the pew singing the hymns. You'll be back to believing something like peace, even in the darkest of times, is a possibility. You'll believe in some long ago promise, forgetting that maybe it wasn't a promise at all, maybe it was lost in translation. Maybe you're wrong. Maybe you went all in on the wrong guy.

"P.S. If you really are fake, don't tell me. I don't want to know."

The Lonely

Alone, all alone
Nobody, but no body
Can make it out here alone.

— Maya Angelou, "Alone"

The Honey Remembers the Honeycomb

Maybe, for you, there is no spray nor scent of the ocean,
     no sugar grains of sand clinging to the fine hairs on your legs,
     your two big toes digging little holes, no hungry boy circling
     lotion on your shoulders, letting his fingers linger there

Maybe there's no sweat on your tongue, no salt in a name
     you haven't heard or spoken in years, a line of letters
     etched onto empty pages that follow the last one you wrote
     it on to say *don't forget to* or *because I love* or *goodbye*

Maybe genetic memory is a myth, the idea that honey
     remembers the hexagonal home of its origin, the belief
     that what was will continue to shape whatever will be. Maybe
     it's another fable of fate when what is, is real, is sweeter.

What Is Your Sign?

Even Sagittarius has a human half, makes a certain sort of sense.
Every sign seems to be lifted from a myth or natural occurrence,
a woman pouring water, a crab, a lion, a bull. The bull of being
the astrological outcast, this chimera without wings or claws or beauty.
The way the listicles call you industrious and loyal, assign you
the leftovers of the list—the least attractive princess or the Chris
they hate on Twitter. When people ask, *What is your sign*?

I take it as an accusation. Like they read me coming in, my button-up
oxford, the pocket square that matched my socks, the way I push
the chairs back into place or disapprove of the loud conversation
in the booth across from us, how nothing is ever quite done, the joy
and the sex are always sufficient or, at least, efficient. I want to make
my case that goats can be gorgeous. But I know who I am. I know
I love lonely cliffs, chewing on scraps, and bleating at passersby.

Friend of the Monster

On his knees, praying for a friend in his terrible loneliness,
the blind man reaches out and touches monstrous flesh, patchwork
of cadavers, of lives like his own, anonymous and empty. "Stay,"
he begs the monster not for his life, not like the others, but for his
company, for a companion in the darkness, someone to sing to.

Believing in what we cannot see is a survival instinct. "Cling,"
they say of the blind, of our *faith*, spit out in derision, a curse
"They *cling* to their—" hope, faith, love, God, whatever accepts
the grip of our need, lets us be of use, lets us more than exist,
lets us matter, even asks us to sing to it, wants to hear us, wants us.

Frankenstein makes himself a monster. Who hasn't been so alone?
Even Christ himself, desperate for fellowship, gathers what lives
he can, asks three to follow him to a garden, in the dark, "Wait,"
he says, knowing they won't, knowing another is gathering silver;
"This flesh is weak, it's true," he reasons, "But their friendship?

I'd die for that."

The Moon in Pisces
Camp Red Cloud, 1996

We had a gold-plated sun, the size of a body
pinned to the living room wall. It was mom's
pride and joy. All of the signs carved in wood,
"I'm the fish, baby," she would tell me, "And,
you and Joseph are half fish." This logic led

me to believe my father a goat, my mother
a double of herself, my twin and I a double
of them both, the sun a true and constant
guide to wherever I was going or wherever
I'd end up.

My body pinned to the earth, the spinning
zodiac, a half dozen airmen trying to lift me.
Perry, holding me, making sure I didn't fall
again or close my eyes, said he looked up
and saw me leaning on the lawnmower,

this handheld ancient thing, just a handle
and blades, we'd been at it so long, pushing
ourselves up the grass covering warheads
older than any of us. He said, "The moon

was just coming over your shoulder. I called
up to you, to look up," he put his hand, a slap
to keep me conscience, "and that's when you
fell, man – you just folded or crumbled up."

Perry had scurried up the side of the mound,
put his face next to my mouth to feel me breathe,
outside of myself, I see my hand reach out to his,
his eyes widen, my lips on his lips, the moon

lifting past him, past him pushing my body back
into the ground, wiping his lips, yelling, "He's okay,"
feeling myself split in two, swim each half away.

Vanilla

Eating too many Nilla Wafers will make the roof of your mouth sting, like tiny wasps are drilling tiny holes into one of the biggest holes you've got.

The tongue is a lick of fire. I spent the summer of my nineteenth birthday eating only Nilla Wafers. It made my mouth hurt. Washed it down with Minute Maid Fruit Punch and didn't put on a pound because I was nineteen and naïve, and sweetness

was something I'd been denied. Or I'd denied myself, even when my roommate broke up with his girlfriend and stumbled back to our barracks, stripped down to his boxers, it was New Year's Eve, said, "I'm not mad at her. I just wish she would've blown me one more time," and he looked at me, like he was focusing on, what?

"You've seen me naked before, right?" and I nodded, looked out of our window at the bakery across the street. It would brighten up at 3 am every morning. They made the best sweet rolls, scent of vanilla wafting into our room. "I have a big dick," he said.

I pretended not to hear him, not to want to see him pull down his boxers. "Get some sleep," I said while fireworks finally hit the sky outside. He moved out the next week. Never talked to me again.

What Used to Be McCarran Airport, Las Vegas

The Spring Mountains out in the distance, if you're lucky
you'll catch a sunset, the diminished edifices of glistening
casinos refracting a little of the glory in their windows
where, once, at what was once The Monte Carlo, we woke,
ordered breakfast after 5 PM, Belgian waffles, strawberries,
crumpled sheets, mounds of whip cream in silver trays,
our pillows piled into a mountain out of the way, grasping
for small talk, you asked me about my Air Force days, sun
almost gone, just a thin red line over the peaks, if I'd ever
slept with another airman, try these strawberries, so sweet,
it wasn't as titillating as you'd expected, you kissed my neck
before I finished the story about a friend, my best friend
then, after a year sitting in my dorm room, whiskey sours,
women he'd loved in Ohio, women he'd liked in between,
driving him to the airport, he looked out at the mountains,
said he hated them, they felt like walls he couldn't climb.

Have You Ever Been So Lonely?
for Rob

Lucy is at the bedside of a stranger, Christmas Eve,
asking him in his coma, guessing probably not, he probably
has a family—Who doesn't have a family?—but Lucy

asks him if he's ever seen a stranger and thought if they knew
you, really knew you, but no, even knocked out in a hospital
he's not the kind who would think like that, think like her.

While You Were Sleeping came out the year of South Korea,
when I pined away for a friend I'd made in Vegas, only a friend,
who wrote me back, almost weekly, he was probably that lonely,

or straight, to somehow miss me falling in love. Maybe I was
lonely, too, convincing myself, sitting with silent photos, letters,
waiting for them to answer, letting them tell me that believing,

against all logic and reason, falling, like a romantic heroine,
was exactly what I was supposed to do in my 20s. When a man
gives you a snow globe, he knows how it feels in there. He knows.

MJ & the Elephant Man

Imagine having to say out loud, "I am not an animal"—
to other homo sapiens, "I am a human being!"

Only place will take you is a place where you are the show
for coins and a bag of peanuts, some toss to you, some
thinking to be cruel, some thinking themselves kind.

It's where you started wearing a hat and a mask. No wonder
he was obsessed, why he wanted to buy your bones (they say).

He'd had brothers, they were *all* the show once, but then
it was just him who kept on changing like Proteus, morphing
into other versions of himself, some people tossed him

their kids, for days, whole weekends, whole weeks
thinking themselves kind, thinking up ways to be cruel.

The things people said, people say, people are animals,
you make them feel, give a thrill, they won't leave you alone.

Where You Got Your Shoes

David should've known when he started talking about a little lamb.
This was going to end up somewhere unexpected. This crafty old
prophet, banging on about a king with all the sheep he could want.
Sheep for days. Sheep for years. *What would you do?* Nathan asks.
What would you do to that man?

Shonna was getting her cards read. Vince was buying a tiny
voodoo doll made of yarn. And there I was, staring dumbly at
the wrought iron balconies, the drunk bridesmaids, college boys
telling one another how this was everything they wanted it to be.
And a bum in a torn tank top says to me, *I bet you $20 I can tell
you where you got your shoes.*

You are that man! The prophet points at David and instantly he
understands *he* was also the lamb sauntering into the trap. You
get so caught up in getting everything you wanted, everything you
maybe think you deserve, you become an easy mark. Temptation
everywhere. A woman bathing on a rooftop. A bet you lost before
you took it.

When you hear the story from another teller, you can't believe it
was you. But you get back to your room, and there's the lamb, and
you're down a twenty. And where the hell are your shoes?

All of My Red Flags Are Heart-Shaped

Kenneth, the pest control guy with the ass, is detailing the way
the poison works. He says that they eat the food but it doesn't kill
them instantly; they live long enough to take it back to the colony
and poison the lot of them. It's early afternoon, the sun still up,
but he takes the beer I offer him and takes a seat. He has a ring.
I remember my mother walking out into traffic when she finally
figured out one of her married men was never getting that divorce.
Kenneth asks if I have another beer, and of course I do.

The One That Got Away

Met him once, Doro's friend from Germany—no specific town,
no history beyond "Peter likes boys, too" and smell of him, raw
and ripe, we were laid out in the sand he put a hand to his eyes,
sunlight slipping past long fingers, his enormous smile at me
pressing my nose into his arm, I wanted to pick him up like
produce, I'd rub my thumb along his forearm, each fine hair aglow.
There are some men who love to touch,

love to be touched; you'd think all of us do, but some start to erect
a radius from birth that reaches further with each encounter, with
each breaking or leaving, learning how to alone ourselves inside
ourselves—but not Peter, who, just meeting me, kissed my cheek at
the airport, said, "Do you like to fuck or be fucked?" and smiled,
"Or both?" put his bag down, I only knew his name and origin,
barely, kissed me again, "Ah, both."

Doro and Dan were talking about their high school days, she the
foreign exchange girl, he the closeted boy she let hold her breasts,
smoke her cigarettes, have the worn copy of Rilke which he read to
me the night before they arrived, "I *have* thought about this," Dan
took a drag, looked into my eyes in that practiced for-an-interview
way, "Me and you, maybe it could work" still looking, another puff,
letting out the smoke in a half smile.

It's imprecise to say I loved him when I can't remember his hands,
or the scent of him, or how he dismissed the idea of *us*, only that
he did, and said Dorothea was bringing Peter who loved Latin
guys, and I was close enough, he'd seen my pictures, a consolation
leaning on his elbows next to me, staring out at our ocean, Dan
and Doro laughing, "It's too bad you're in love with him," Peter
didn't look at me, just, "I'd like to fuck you."

These Gays Are Trying to Murder Me
on The White Lotus

This time it's Sicily,
but Tanya returns, a new husband
from the last season says she's so fat
is maybe why he can't get it up.

You gotta hate this guy. The clues,
everyone knows after the fact, obvious
from the first chants and the frescos
of mortals buggered by the gods.

Seeing the Essex kid follow suit
with his uncle, "I wanted gay sex,"
the writer said, "to be transgressive
again," and there she is, a white

negligee, following the animal sound,
I think they hear when I come out,
on a first meeting, at an interview. She
says, "I don't think that's his uncle"

but her assistant doesn't understand,
it's hard to explain how I knotted up
watching this guy, barely a man, go
at it, trancelike, and I thought about

Sergio taking me to the wall in Rome
where, all of seventeen, he let a guy
bow to him and worship, and Shane
at the bar, on the same trip to Italy,

let this old man hold his crotch, smiled
at me and said I should loosen up, but
kept on losing me to call his own boy,
while I found myself far away and alone.

She was right. Eventually. Too late,
"You'll end up in some crazy places, right?"
the dark water, this gorgeous, horrifying
swathe of sea, "But you'll still be lost."

Another Look at Lonely

"Don't buy a house," my friend says. We are parked outside of my apartment. Dinner was lovely, but he told his husband he wanted to drive me home. "I don't know how much more I can take," the house has been under construction for three years, their daughter is in her grating teens, and his husband, who he has called *Sunshine* since he introduced us so many years ago, just keeps believing everything will work itself out. "It's like I am the only one worried, the only one looking ahead." My friend came here from Mexico with nothing, less than nothing—not even the language. I understand how terrifying it is. To a point. A *regular* home would never take three years. They are building a mansion. That's not an exaggeration. My friend built a life for himself with his own hands, sure, but it got a big damn upgrade with Sunshine. Sunshine gave him a home with *two* dishwashers just for the hell of it, and a toilet that talks to you and washes your ass. Sunshine wants to send their daughter to an expensive school in Boston. He doesn't mind taking out a loan or two. "He says he has a plan," and I ask my friend if his husband's plans ever work out. "Sure, but it's different this time." When they brought me to the place they bought, before they started knocking out walls, I said *Holy Shit* and meant it. I ask my friend if he'd like to come upstairs for some tea, but he says he has to get back. "We need to hang out more," he says, like he always does, but I am always the one calling. And it's Sunshine who invited me to dinner. I start the teapot in this apartment I rent. Owning is overrated.

I Wasn't Finished

Mourning or pretending. Just one more
hour for Miami, listening to the raucous
revelers necking and pawing their way
down to the ocean, watching the fireworks
while you slept, oblivious to it all—

A balcony at the Hard Rock, waiting on dawn,
trying not to take one last look at you, your
naked soles, calves, thighs, all those marathons
for an ass that doesn't quit, the plane of back
blade to blade, no space for me. I can't quit

reaching. We know the answer before we ask.
There is too much wisdom, too much damage
to be impressed by how it fell so easy, just
another idol body, to lose oneself again, and
again. There's a relic of me in Mexico, kissing

the wind, a man, air in my hand. One in Rome
says to read him something that cleaves me
as he drives deep the chisel, the hidden tang
thrumming the handle in his hand. I wasn't
finished praying at the altar of artifacts, pieces

of us where I left the oddments, looking for
you to call me back to bed, you to be there, for
a way to see you clumsy men, your wreckage, you
and me as *intended*. Excavation is a belief that
there is more to see beneath the rubble and debris.

Before the Afterworld

*Dearly Beloved, we are gathered here today
to get through this thing called life.*

— *Prince, "Let's Go Crazy"*

Somebody said, "Let's have a *Purple Rain* viewing party!" and
there we were, a few days later, crammed into a friend's apartment
sipping "Raspberry berets," a candy-sweet concoction I'd dreamt
up to use up my Cointreau and Chambord leftover from the
Christmas shindig (when David projectile vomited on Marty's cat;
everyone thought it was *the best* of our get togethers). Big plastic
bowls of popcorn and chips being passed around like offering
plates. Pappy lecturing someone in the kitchen about who knows
what. Richelle and Lenice putting whip cream on the Jell-O shots,
Richelle telling Pappy, "Can't you see he doesn't want to hear that?"
and hands our "old man" a shot, kiss on the cheek, too... that's
how she was. How we all were. A golden age, so brief and glowing,
we somehow knew to lavish each moment in joy and affection. The
alcohol helped.

Michael and Chandra, always the main event where they went,
were up at every music riff, grinding in front of the widescreen,
Michael doing his tongue-out, finger snap sexy/gross thing, and
Chan telling everyone at the top of her voice, "I *love* you guys!"

Some 25 years hence, I'm running a trail in my Dallas suburbs and
"Let's Go Crazy" shifts into the playlist. In the movie, Prince takes
the stage, owns it. The fog and the backlight are ethereal, then the
guitar comes in. It wasn't long after the party when life started
to happen, pick us off the scene bit by bit. New jobs, marriages,
scandals, eventually some kids, more and more distance, more and
more promises to get together, fewer and fewer follow throughs.

Sometimes I start running and I can't stop, I don't notice the sun
setting, skin too hot to feel the chill of the evening. Then it hits me,
what effort it is going to take to get back. It's usually a slow go of it.
Or, if you're lucky, a song will take you there.

It's called Golden Age Thinking (according to Michael Sheen's character in *Midnight in Paris*), this belief that some other time was better than the present. We were all mostly poor, infighting, I was jealous of almost everyone, we often felt lost and lonely, some of us were directionless, some suffering unknown and unspeakable wounds in a crushing silence. In other words, not much different from wherever any adult finds themselves today.

There are moments, in this new life with my new friends, when I feel that same inkling I felt back then, the desire to somehow preserve that moment. Back then, I took hundreds of pictures (most of them lost because they were physical photos), tried to write down what I remembered over hangover coffee. But the people of this life have their own Golden Ages, and we catch each other traveling back at the very moments we should be cataloguing the present. Maybe this has always been the case.

Maybe I can't recall *all* of the Purple Rain Party because there were instances when I was back at a high school dance getting lost in "I Would Die 4 U" or weeping over "When Doves Cry"—the chorus, *How could you just leave me standing alone in a world that's so cold?*

Back then, there was always someone who'd answer the phone, join you for a trip to Panda Express or some other cheap excuse for company. We'd get off work, order a pizza, go to someone's house to debate which Janet Jackson album was *the best* or solve our friends' relationship problems with *American Idol* playing in the background, Ryan Seacrest narrating the drama on screen and off. I put the song on repeat for the run home.

Let's go crazy.

I think of Adam losing it on a guest, screaming, his face getting redder and redder.

Let's get nuts.

Tito scheming to sell stuff from work on the burgeoning internet market.

This life, you're on your own.

I miss them all so much. Seems such a foolish thing to say. But I know so many who don't look back with anything but scorn. They have their reasons, I am sure. Maybe the real pain comes with knowing you can't ever go back. It'll break you down trying.

If you don't like the world you're living in—

It's not that I want to go back there necessarily.

Take a look around—

I just don't want to lose those moments before the Afterworld (as Prince called it). To lose *them,* the people I picked up along the way who make it bearable.

At least you got friends.

I get back to my apartment, send a text to Pappy and Marty (the only two I keep any sort of regular contact; months pass between these messages, sometimes years): "Raspberry Berets next time we meet" attach a YouTube link to the whole soundtrack playlist. Two hearts, almost immediately.

Cope
for Jeff Albers

Who by aspersions throw a stone
At th' head of others, hit their own.

— George Herbert, "Charms and Knots"

"Professor Isip," my student is a little angry, holding up her laptop to me, a wiki for David Foster Wallace, the bandana photo, "You didn't tell us he *killed himself*?"

It's not the first time a student has confronted me about this. I've assigned Wallace's 2005 Kenyon graduation speech, "This Is Water," for well over a decade. Generally, maybe because these are freshmen who need something to believe in, maybe because it's just *that* good, they fall in love. And, as they do, they dive all the way in—want to know everything about him.

"Does that make a difference?" I ask, still curious myself.

She is shocked, "Yes!" She thinks about what to say, "I'm not saying he's bad for killing himself. I know… I have a friend" she wrote about this friend in her first paper. There's a lot of them who have a high school friend who committed suicide. A lot of them want to write about it.

When *Infinite Jest* came out, I didn't know who David Foster Wallace was or that he was *important*. I was at a military base in Turkey trying not to be gay. When I went back to get my MA, it was 2008. I was in Dr. Bonca's class getting ready to talk about postmodernism when he sat down at the front table and cried. He'd met him. Maybe they were friends, I can't remember. I just know he meant *that* much to Bonca.

Wallace opens the speech with a story about two fish swimming and an older fish asks them, "How's the water?" They wait for the older fish to pass and ask one another, "What the hell is water?"

"But if you're worried that I plan to present myself here as the wise older fish explaining what water is to you younger fish, please don't be," though this is *exactly* what Wallace does for the next twenty or so minutes of the speech. I let my students listen to the speech in class. Recently, I've picked up on the eeriness of listening to the dead.

A large part of graduate school, for me, was bitching about how postmodernists got it all wrong. What the fuck did all of that deconstruction have to offer any of us after September 11th? Sometimes students ask me about 9-11 like it's some far off time recorded in a textbook, certainly nothing the living know about firsthand, "How did you get over it?"

These days they mean September 11th, but they also mean what should have been their formative years spent locked inside, spent behind a mask, spent stuck. I think of President Bush saying we needed to go to Walt Disney World to beat the terrorists, so we went. We got back to living. We pantomimed what we remembered about living.

Almost five years later, Wallace gives this speech at Kenyon. It "goes viral," or whatever the equivalent of that was in 2005. In academia, the postmodernists were aware of the crumbling support for their ways and their work. You don't need a young scholar to tell you that you're old news. Whatever this new thing was didn't have a name. Maybe *post*-postmodernism. The New Sincerity? Some have settled on Metamodernism. But I liked "The New Sentimental."

"How do you get over it?" my students want to know about moving past all these lost years.

The morning the towers fell, I was just getting to work at Disneyland. We weren't going to open, of course, but there were all of these families basically trapped in the hotels. They couldn't leave, and they couldn't go to the parks. All their excited kids just wanted to get on rides, they had no idea the world was ending.

The foods folks made these elaborate baskets of Mickey-shaped cookies, muffins, croissants, really heavy fruit. Each of us would join a few characters, I was with Snow White and Winnie the Pooh, and knock on the doors of the guests. The kids were all screams and hugs, the parents kept looking back at the television screens. Snow White would kneel down to every kid, even the taller but terrified twelve-year-olds, and say, "I know what it's like to be afraid" and then she'd tell them her fairy tale, a condensed version for some… an elaborate version for others.

When we got back to the golf cart, two baskets empty, Snow White put her head in her hands and cried. Pooh took his head off and massaged her shoulders.

"I don't know how you get over it," I tell my students, "I honestly don't know if you ever *do* get over it. I'm just an English professor. All I know to do, all that's ever worked for me is to write it down. Tell your story."

Some of them try to bury the lead, nearly a page of description before anything happens. Others want to tell me statistics about all the dead, from the plague and from the suicides and from being in the wrong place at the wrong time. One of my creative writing students says, "Professor Isip, do you think this is too hokey?" He's one of the best in the class, grandson, or great-grandson of Larry McMurtry. "I don't want to come off as too sentimental."

Wallace was known for these meandering ideas that would try to distance the reader from the moment. As he's being repulsed at a cruise ship buffet or a porn convention autograph booth, he drops in some random facts to draw the gaze away from his visceral reactions. If you were looking for the signs, you might have picked up on a guy refusing to own what he was feeling, or even who he was.

"Did you know he was an abuser?" another student asks me, again the accusing tone.

This, of course, has made me reconsider using the speech. I reason I'd have to cut out a whole lot of my readings if I had to cut every fucked-up writer; I don't know a writer or an academic or a person in general who isn't a little fucked up. I suppose that is what the kids would call "cope," and maybe it is.

"Yes. I can assign you something different if you like," I offer. Nobody has ever taken me up on this. None of them bring it up in their papers. I don't think it's because it doesn't matter. I think it's because, like me in Turkey, they've got other shit on their minds. And, again, they tend to like what he's saying in the speech. They don't write about his suicide either.

He keeps driving home the point that we have a *choice* about how we see the world. We can deconstruct the life of a dead man, psychoanalyze his relationships, come to the conclusion that everything and everyone is fucked-up or, worse, meaningless. You can give in to the nihilism or depression. You can drink or get high, screw your brains out. Hang yourself. Or…

When she finally composed herself, Snow White asked Pooh to hand her the makeup bag. She looked at herself in her compact, "How many more stops do we have?"

I didn't want to say it, "That was only the first floor. We aren't even finished with this hotel. I just wanted to get you out here for a break."

She laughed, that way between sincerity and madness, "Well, let's go back in" dropping the lipstick back into the bag, "I'd rather be Snow White than me right now."

The New Sentimental was, if I remember correctly, something about a return to belief. That if all these decades of postmodernity had revealed something "more real" than the real, then maybe there was something beyond that, like Plato's Realm of Forms. Like heaven. Like something to believe in.

She'll be Snow White because you need her to be Snow White. He'll be the David Foster Wallace of the 2005 speech because you need that version of him. Because you have a choice of how you see this world.

And maybe that's cope. And maybe that's okay.

The Leaving

You need not die today.
Stay here—through pout or pain or peskyness.
Stay here. See what the news is going to be tomorrow.

— Gwendolyn Brooks, "To the Young Who Want to Die"

Ode to Frito Pie

If you call it pie, it's pie. Like a regime that sprung up overnight,
nobody asking about bodies they know not to ask about, little flags
to celebrate the agreed upon thing, you accept what you are served.

Split the bag right down the side so it becomes a cup of corn chips,
an ingenious efficiency, like the monkey skull in *Temple of Doom*
that doubled as a dish for its chilled brain, just add chili and cheese.

We had it at Dan's funeral with bottles of *Shiner*, added white onion
to joke about the tears, to laugh at anyone asking why you call it pie,
grateful for a question we could answer among many we could not.

It Won't Break My Heart to Say Goodbye

What was this world but a crumbling stucco edifice
and the green glass shards from a last call drunk
staggering in every direction but home?

When did it offer more than just enough to keep on
existing, a fuel spill shimmering in the wake of morning
after morning, alarms instead of birdsongs?

Why should I miss it?
Why would I miss it?
Why would it miss me?
Why should it miss me?

Was I known for planting seeds or pruning branches,
for leaving sugared water for the hummingbirds,
or offering soft words to those in need of them?

What was I but another machine leaving tire tread tracks
over the homes and humans and habitats in my way,
the exhaust of my thoughts polluting the air?

How can we know
what we will miss
when we miss so
much and we
know even
less?

Every Party

Brings me back to our kitchen in the projects.
Cow curtains and magnets lining the yellow
refrigerator packed with food we couldn't eat
for almost a week. Instead, we made meals
of leftover meat and veg from the lumpia,
mom up all night cutting and frying, all of us
dreaming of the grand entrance, "Let them

call us poor when they see this!" Every dish
a brick balanced in the façade, a challenge
to notice they were the cheap cuts and donations,
she had a gift for flavor no one could deny it,
until she didn't, until, like so much of this life
it left her in the lurch without her last defense
there would be no more hiding, "Let them

say what they want!" and they did, *she* did,
my sister, tasting the fruit salad of canned fruit
and marshmallows, condensed milk, coconut,
what we had left in the cupboards, everything
mom could think of, everything but an apology,
so who could blame the cruelty, "Let them

take it back with them" my sister wasn't trying
to cover her voice, "It's terrible, you don't want
to try it" she said, I couldn't see to who, but heard
every word sitting next to mom who pulled in
her bottom lip the way she did when life hit her,
or a husband, or a daughter who maybe had a right,
maybe she thought, *I deserve it*, chin out, "Let them."

Phantom Limbs

When Mom lost her fingers, I had a clinical curiosity
about what she felt, if when she reached out to hug me
she could feel her fingers press my back like I still can,
like I still do all of these years after I lost the rest of her.

This phenomenon is repeating. Dad is losing extremities
of everyone he sees, his children only the largest shadow
through the gauze and haze, only floating bodies, lolling
heads like they were when he held them, when he held us

so long ago, it all looked so clear to him, the years ahead,
the way we'd grow, even outgrow his vision, her touch,
our need for them. It is impossible to lose a part of you
and move as if it were not there, still there, reaching out.

Giraffe Tattoo

Did I leave them on her nightstand?

What I didn't know would be the last day,
Mom handed me two sheets of college rule
paper, the frayed edges from the coil binding
losing bits like baby teeth.

In streaks of blue ballpoint ink, imprecise
lines that indicate this is only a draft, she'd
probably taken hours, days even to sketch
two pictures: a giraffe with palm trees and

Jesus looking just past the broken edges.

It had been a good day. She told me about
saving some money, maybe $50, for a home,
just a small apartment. She said you can move
in with me, baby. I didn't say I'd rather die.

She'd given me this gold pendant of Jesus
that she'd bought for one of her ex-husbands,
or he'd bought it for her. I sold it for rent, or
a car repair. She weighed worth by what you gave.

I gave her an occasional Saturday afternoon.

With what was left of her right hand, she held
out a wad of $10 bills before I left. I'm not
getting no damn apartment, she said, I'll die
here. I must have laid her art down to take

the money she had scrounged away. No, you
won't I said, but she did. Mom, you're gonna
live forever, drawing stuff, like this giraffe.
It's your favorite animal, baby. I didn't say

It wasn't. Now, here's my body, penance.

Golden Dreams
at Disney California Adventure

Appropriate it didn't last long. History
is not what theme park people come for.
The opposite, really. Escape from history,
to zing past yourself into a stratosphere
of make-believe. It's why Hollywood,
the place I lost myself in a hotel room
at sixteen with big dreams of dancing,

stupid enough to believe some producer
saw something in me, how he said it, "You
are something special" and kept repeating
special, special into my ear, I could feel
the blood and the lube and the producer
special, special, calls out to lonely boys
come sell yourself, be bigger, *special*—

Golden Dreams told the story of California,
the whitest "natives" they could pay, Whoopi
was Califia, "the spirit of this place," showing
up at the dam with Mulholland, on the cliff
where a Chinese man and his son, bamboo hats
of course, scream up to pull their basket from
the exploding rock, out of the smoke, here
comes Whoopifia, "It wasn't always easy

for folks," a part that park guests complained
about, it was too depressing to think of dying
or even other people long dead just when you
were digesting a frozen lemonade and churro,
it was all too much reality when you'd brought
the kids for a day to be a cowboy or a princess,
to be something *special*—

The producer sent my mom three checks, each
for $300, enough for rent or food, so who was I
to stop meeting him, here was water in a dry land,
who was I to pull on the rope, to scream "pull me
up," here was where I belonged, face into the rock
getting packed in with explosives, who the fuck
was I, someone special?

Frog and Toad Are Friends
for Arnold Lobel

In the brown-green forest of cattails and snails
wandering past a diminutive fence, the final slat
swinging, sit two friends chatting.

Two friends chatting about a dragonfly one saw
skip the pond showing off how one might cause
a ripple, make a stir. Toad can't

bring himself to touch the water, so he stirs sugar
in his tea, and listens to his friend, his buoyant friend
always nearby, always within reach.

"I really don't quite know what I'm doing," Frog
confessed once, and Toad replied, "Some part of you
knows." But his friend thought, "No, really not."

There were hikes, small adventures, silences. Frog
left a note telling his friend, "I want to be alone"
and Toad took a turtle to find him.

The turtle asked, "Why don't you leave him alone?"
Do you say, without a friend, this world is too much
for me? No, not *a* friend. Without Frog.

Frog sitting out there on a rock, watching a dragonfly,
like the one his friend was so enamored with, just
a touch will disturb the still waters.

Past the Crickets in the Tall Summer Grass
San Pedro, 1992

We are out of breath, soaked in sweat and dew. Anthony can't stop laughing, the moon spotlights his white chest. We all shed our shirts and shorts, Cody's letterman jacket he's only had for months. All lost in the sand and the grass, somewhere between the Korean Friendship Bell and the highway where we are waiting for Cody's mom, down to our underwear. Before we could ring it, there was rustling behind us. Then the blinding skunk smell in our mouths and throats and eyes. We tried our best to outrun it. Tried our best to keep down the pregame wine coolers and cheese sticks. I wanted to turn back for the jacket; I spent three months' pay on it. Even though I knew it was ruined. Cody turned me around, pointed at Anthony in the moonlight, twirled his finger to his temple, *I think he's lost it!* When his mom pulled up, she said, "I could see all of you naked a mile away" and she kept saying, "None of you better throw up in my car." I don't know how all of us, nearly men, squeezed into the tub, when and how the cans of tomato sauce got opened or poured on us. I just remember rinsing it all off, the skunk, the tomato bits, the shards of grass. Anthony and Cody, towels around their waists, recounting the bell, the skunk, and the shoes we shucked. Something else was missing. The graduation ring Cody bought me, just a little loose on my finger. *Where did it slip off?* I'd had it for such a short time. Every now and then I think of going back to find it. They say a bell can't be unrung, but what if you never got to ring it?

The Twilight Zone

It is the middle ground between light and shadow,
between science and superstition, let us allow
ourselves the luxury of another dimension
somewhere you and I, perhaps, may envision
a better life, a better *us* than what we know.

You don't cheat. I don't leave. You and I, we don't go
down opposing roads; instead, we stay, instead, we grow.
You and I, we find another way, make another decision;
it is the middle ground between light and shadow.

Between the pit of man's fears, like losing or letting go,
and the summit of our knowledge, how you know I know
that this is a fifth dimension, beyond logic or reason,
vast as space, the scope of a hope long past its season
sees infinity, a road that reconnects, lets us pass, lets us grow;
it is the middle ground.

The Last Time I Told a Man I Loved Him, I Didn't Know I Didn't Mean Love, Didn't Mean Him

Confessing never guarantees absolution, but at least there is the momentary self-forgiveness we call acceptance, even *growth*. Even if we know the truth. Even if passing an apartment with the same number in a town four states away and fourteen years on brings a pang somewhere deep where who you believe you are meets who you were. And you were cruel, of course. His hands, you remember, were wide and empty, like his eyes, like all the years since. Whenever you hear the old Bonnie Raitt song, you think of what he might have said if given the chance to say anything at all.

Departing, Chicago
for Scott

Six-dollar cider, Styrofoam cup already
disintegrating, between the beanie and scarf,
that look, tears gathered to crow's feet,
denying the season is almost over. It was

Autumn the first time, Insta-worthy elk
lumbering at the park, at the Bean, a thumb
peeks into the frame so clear one could fall
into and love its intricacies. But now

"The duck was better." The one I ordered,
cherry reduction, crisp brussels, rare, "Take mine"
after you asked the waiter if that was truffle oil
a third time. The pear tart was exhausting.

Determined, like a country song or a Windy
City wind unphased by pea coat, sweater,
skin, *not the right time* you said but pulled
nearer. At O'Hare, our kiss is embarrassing

like teenagers leaving summer camp, passing
some meager memento—sunglasses, lanyard,
promises, hope. "It was good to see you,"
I didn't expect the cold. No coat. "Take mine."

...

How strange to see them, every time a blaze
cuts across California, a tornado in Texas,
those damaged and desperate refugees take
singed teddy bears, photo albums spilling

neglected pages, family and lovers forgotten
long before this present destruction, before this
too familiar tableau, a look over the shoulder
at everything, *everything* we cannot take away.

A Scarf for the Statue

In front of the student hall where we would drink
pitchers of beer on January nights before football
practice spilled out the hometown heroes, stands
a statue of a once famous judge wearing his robe,
holding his gavel midair, and mounds of snow
pile at his shoes and in the creases of his sleeves.

Donna, a year before retiring, decided to knit a scarf
in the school colors, and late afternoons in sunset shadows
I'd see her at it like Penelope, each looping motion a making
or an unmaking, some final order in the chaos of threads or
some first rattle of feathers shaking off a season so long
she'd started to look at her feet, how still they'd become.

You Say You're Suicidal

Subtraction looks like addition,
in the frame of this photo you
are always blocking out the sun
so much brighter than you—

Remember looking right into it,
when you looked away, shut eyes
still shining tiny suns in the dark
like you saved it, multiplied it

just being there, as if you were
meant to be there to capture it all
with your unique vision, as if you
were the prism where the light

breaks into color, where the sun
would have bleached it all out,
each detail of this picture of you
preserving the world being there,

in the frame, in the way, being there.

Straight for the Bear

In 2021, seventeen soldiers took their own lives in Alaska, a location with a paltry 11,000 or so on the bases. The funny thing is that nobody seemed to think of this as a tragedy or at least an anomaly.

So many people had died these last few years, and soldiers in particular, many new to a gun and new to wherever the United States government had placed them, and new to solitude. Well, it wasn't uncommon.

Still, some official somewhere made the call, "Get your shit together!"

By the time my brother, an Army Chaplain, arrived, there had already been two more deaths. Joseph called me when he got there, "I already hate this place."

Joseph took the assignment because the money was good, and because he thought he could do some good there. He wasn't fond of his first trip; we both hated the cold, and that first time he was there in the dead of it. He said he finally understood why I was so miserable in South Korea, how the cold and the constant gray skies got you too much in your head.

This coming from a philosophy major.

Just before these orders, he was doing chaplain work at UCLA Medical Center. Driving past the homeless encampments, he'd call me for a distraction, "I haven't had any sleep. Last night I got called in because one of the kids on my floor wasn't going to make it," he was in the pediatric hospice area or something like that, a place where kids go to die, "When I got there, the nurse on duty walked me in, everyone was crying obviously, but they all just stopped and looked at me. They do this crap all the time."

He meant the nurses or the doctors, the hospital. They walked these spiritual advisors into the room, be it hope or spite, they almost push them forward as if to say, "Fix it!"

"What did they say?"

I meant the family, the suffering. Maybe they, too, were thinking, "Can you? Fix it?"

"Nothing! Absolutely nothing. They just kept staring at me," he laughed a little, "I told them I would be in the hallway if they need to talk or pray. It was *awkward*."

"I can't even imagine," but of course I could. There was a lot I could imagine. I could absolutely imagine what all of those soldiers in Alaska were thinking.

The highest rates of suicide in the United States are those over 75… and those between 25 and 34, the age of most of those soldiers. Both groups see everyone they know dying.

"You said your friend in Vegas, the sergeant, he did it with a gun, right?" Joseph isn't sentimental like me. He doesn't bring up the past all the time. But he didn't really forget things either. I had only mentioned Sarge once or twice.

"Yeah. Brian was the one who found him," Brian couldn't give you even the most basic details without choking up. Even now, some thirty years later.

"One of my guys," we're back to Alaska, "He keeps talking about his weapon."

"And you can't tell anyone?"

He laughed, "*Of course*, I can! And I did! This is the US Army; I get paid to *tell someone*." The soldier would go through a counseling regimen. In a few months, maybe weeks, he'd get a clean bill of health. And he'd get his weapon back.

It's hard to recruit and harder to retain these days. Two whole generations watched uncles and brothers come back completely broken, and nobody knew who or what or why they were fighting, or even if a war was happening anywhere.

"Four more soldiers," I was watching an episode of *The Great British Baking Championship* when he called, and they were hugging the old guy being sent home. "Three of them were here, right on my base."

My brother is not dramatic. He wasn't trying to shock me, just sharing. I said, "Are you okay?"

"What? Oh, yeah. You get used to," he stopped himself, "I don't mean you get used to it. I mean" thinking about it, "I mean I'm fine."

Magen and the kids went out to visit him for this trip. If you were going to be in Alaska, you should go when it's not cold—which is a pretty short window. They did it up, went everywhere with a dot on the map. He sent me pictures of Sarah feeding reindeer and Joshua smiling outside of a fence, an oblivious bear far in the background.

A selfie of him and Magen and some beautiful lake behind them. They were smiling, but my brother looked so old. My twin looked so much older than me.

"How much longer do you have?" It was nearly November. In another week or so, the division leaders would finally send an open letter to acknowledge the suicides were not slowing down.

"One week. Thank God," the Army was throwing everything and nothing at the problem. Chaplains cycling in and out, counselors, civilian consultants who charged them top dollar because it's the US military and a guaranteed check.

My brother, a good soldier, would never say what I would say, "They are going to FUBAR this like everything else."

But he could agree, "You're not wrong."

My brother likes to go for long runs like me. Actually, he's kinda the reason I started doing them. He'd tell me about running in Alaska, "You get used to the deer, but you see elk or a bear, and you remember everything out there is trying to kill you."

I'd laugh and say I would *never* run out there, "That's what treadmills are for! I'm not fucking with an elk or a goddamn bear!"

Not missing a beat, "Sure you would. You remember Korea, you did so many crazy things there. Why?"

I've spent thirty years trying to forget Korea, and the military. Trying to forget the cold between the ages of 25 and 34. The teeth and claws and heft of the animals.

"Because I didn't care."

"That's right," he doesn't talk about his dead soldiers or complain about how inept the Army is. He just says, "I can see you running straight for the bear."

Writing Against Oblivion
for Donna

> *like the fragrance of blossoming trees*
> *that grows stronger after*
> *you've passed them*

> — Dorianne Laux, "I Dare You"

Finally caught Donna and Mike for dinner before their annual
trip to Paris. They are doing retirement right. We're not even
two drinks down, and Donna, who recruited me to my doctoral
program, is tearing up. She and Mike are talking about her mentor,
David Bartholomae, who has just passed. In between their own
grad school tales (When the last Boomers are gone, will we even
know if hitchhiking was actually a thing or something they made
up?), Donna tells me and Khimen, "You are my legacy, all of you"
and she means it.

Every time a student sits down to write for us, he has to invent
the university for the occasion—invent the university, that is, or a
branch of it, like History or Anthropology or Economics or English.
He has to learn to speak our language, to speak as we do, to try
on the peculiar ways of knowing, selecting, evaluating, reporting,
concluding, and arguing that define the discourse of our community.

Oteshima has lost its final child. There's a graduation ceremony
for one, and everyone who can make it is here to wish her well.
They are outnumbered by the disinterested cats who being cats,
the mediums of death, are rarely roused by decimation. Akino
Imanaka, at only 15, has the unenviable task of keeping her home
alive in whatever she remembers about it and whatever she decides
to share of that memory. The one-page CBS News article about
Akino's graduation tells us that Oteshima "faces almost certain
oblivion."

I've only taught in this college English department for ten years, which is slight by comparison to many folks my age in their chosen profession. Yet, at almost fifty, I'm among the younger crowd. A dozen colleagues have retired boasting 28- and 30-year-long tenures. Peggy, after losing her husband, went to live a life she'd been putting off. Delores posts weekly pictures of her with her grandkids in Washington. Scott keeps threatening to hang it up and leave the school's lit mag to me.

We think of legacy as a gift. But the family photo albums, the porcelain knickknacks, the quilt fraying at the edges, and the stultifying prospect of spending our remaining years trying to keep the threads from spinning out, the stories in order… it's a burden, too. Thank you for the mahogany China cabinet, mom! *How the fuck am I gonna get this up the stairs?*

The students have to appropriate (or be appropriated by) a specialized discourse, and they have to do this as though they were easily and comfortably one with their audience, as though they were members of the academy, or historians or anthropologists or economists; they have to invent the university by assembling and mimicking its language.

Elliot Haspel, in a 2021 article about the United States' birth rate in "unyielding decline," likens the phenomenon to an asteroid. We will join the ranks of Japan, Italy, Finland, and Norway in what seems like a collective acceptance of extinction. An article in today's *The Economist* says it's getting worse.

Some colleagues died before retiring. Sean with a nearly imperceptible, then untreatable brain illness. From Geology, Patrick, who I barely knew, a gay man living with his dog, seemingly everything to live for, couldn't endure the solitude and paranoia of the pandemic. Chris was in a hospital for such a short window, my mentor, Tony, by his side. When he moved to another campus, Tony said, "There are ghosts here, J.D." I see them everywhere. Or, I *want* to see them everywhere. I miss their company. Or, I miss the possibility of their company, the unexpected office visit, the wave in the hallway, the invitation to a drink or dinner I put off offering.

If we are honest, we all want to be ghosts. I haven't met an atheist so convinced of the worm-food hypothesis that he refrains from the argument. What is the point of arguing any point at all if you believe, *really* believe that it ultimately does not matter? We want to speak or write ourselves into eternity. After all, for so many of us, it is only in the end that we have picked up anything worth passing on. Most of this life is faking it, a bluff.

They must learn to speak our language. Or they must dare to speak it, or to carry off the bluff, since speaking and writing will most certainly be required long before the skill is "learned." And this, understandably, causes problems.

It is summer 2023. There are headlines about orcas forming in groups, attacking boats in the Strait of Gibraltar. A military whistleblower says the United States is hiding alien crafts and *actual aliens* from the public. People are worried about whether or not we'll have another Trump presidency. We are certain, some say, to fall to our robot overlords forming under the benevolent guise of helpful artificial intelligence. Once again, it seems, the world is ending.

Adam Smith says, "Man naturally desires, not only to be loved, but to be lovely; or to be that thing which is the natural and proper object of love." My colleague from Economics, Michael, recommended I get into Smith. Michael spent his sowing oats years building homes in third-world countries, the kind of guy who thinks about the environment, the future, what his boys will think of him and the world he left to them. Of course, we want them to see us better than we are; according to Smith, we dread "not only blame, but blameworthiness; or to be that thing which, though it should be blamed by nobody, is, however, the natural and proper object of blame." A parent, a mentor, an English professor.

Donna and Mike are back in Paris this summer. Scott, Tony, and Michael are all away on vacation. I'm here, a gay man living with my dogs, seemingly everything to live for. Writing against oblivion.

What is generally true about writing… it is an act of aggression disguised as an act of charity.

The Living

Dust thou art, and dust returnest,
Was not spoken of the soul.

— Henry Wadsworth Longfellow, "A Psalm of Life"

Hyperion: 800 Years a Redwood

All the history you know looks different from here
where the air is thin, where the view is clearer. I see
concrete and tarmac arteries, sure, but from here
evergreen forests, patches of vegetable farms, wide
stretches of palmed deserts, a deeper, vaster ocean
even than you might imagine. You might imagine

this world is too much, mountain peaks too high
and valleys dug too terribly deep, much too much
to take in or take on in a lifetime, but what do you
use to measure a life? Once in a lifetime, they said,
about the wars, the crumbling towers, the newest
disease and the billions of bodies. Once in a life

is enough to witness it all, to watch the little ones
you knew from acorns burn at your feet, cut down
in their prime, their strong bodies used to build
an alien forest that glows and buzzes and outgrows
everything here that knows you have to take time
to be that strong, to stand it all you have to stand

longer than you think you can, maybe even alone
save for the creatures who occasionally make you
a home, birth their young and their dreams, move on
leaving only their scattered feathers, the scratches in
your skin, the memory of their movements, the peace
of their sleeping bodies resting in this awkward body

you managed, somehow, to keep living in spite of it
all. All of history, all of us are only a mystery growing
more enigmatic and majestic the longer we persist.
Live a little longer, I want to tell them, the tiny bodies
climbing out of their cars, scrambling up to me in awe
and bursting into tears because I seem impossible.

What You Catch

I was never afraid before you showed up.

— Bill, *The Last of Us*

It catches you off-guard how easily he got in
past the barricades and traps, the flamethrowers
and the carefully placed trips and triggers,
a man in a hole waiting for a hand or a bullet.

We've fallen in love with dystopias for years
because we were looking for a reason to live
through the everyday wastelands, our zombie
days and fungal existence persists in shadows.

You've survived the loneliness, the jackboot
government fucks, and, miraculously, a once-
in-a-century pandemic. "Living in," Ronstadt sang,
"a love that never was." Then he falls into the pit

you dug, looks like someone you'd want, want to
help up. You get a ladder, everyone in this world
wants to kill you, you know, but you let it down.
People are mad your lives didn't move the story along.

Two men giggling like girls in a patch of strawberries
"I can't say you hurt me," They grow old, these men
we never were, finally die, "When you never let me
near..." Together in this rotting and murderous world.

Winter Wonderland

There's a mechanical Mrs. Claus and Santa, each with a small
light for their candles as if they were at a front porch ready to
carol whoever opened the door to them, as if that is what we do,
naturally, open up—

Mom bought them on clearance from Gemco, the year she had
work at Helen Grace Chocolates, let us have the fresh toffee bars,
strawberries she'd just dipped, the three-layered truffles she made
better than anyone.

It was the year they knocked her off the bus stop bench, all the
money and the government check, all of the days in the sweets
shop, long nights at Sav-on, where she'd put some stuffed elephants
on layaway for us,

all of it running off down Via Wanda Avenue, Mom screaming for
help and nobody coming. She just stopped, walked back home,
didn't cry, just said we'd better pray as hard as we could because
she couldn't anymore.

People don't believe me. About the nurses who took up donations,
brought us board games and Christmas dinner. About my brother
Sam and his friend begging the tree lot to give us some almost
dead thing nobody was gonna buy.

About why I listen to Christmas music sometimes six months out
of the year, same songs from the 80s, Larry Groce on the Disney
Christmas album, was singing "Sleigh Ride" with Mickey on one of
Mom's only lucky nights. Belief.

It all seems too perfect, they say. Too Hallmark. How it all comes
together, like they missed the part of Mom's scraped knees, the
year we let ourselves in, ate only candy she snuck us after a long
day gone. What's hard to believe?

Kindness

Sometimes you have to be the one pushing in the blade,
a turn to the right, a turn to the left, make sure the thing
doesn't suffer.

Or, though it kills you and you're sure you can't, you will
stay silent long enough for the lesson to sink in, helplessly
watch the struggle from afar.

Sometimes, looking at old photos, what you once loved is
gone, and you walk back through time like a detective, try
to determine what was cruel, what was kind.

A Mustard Seed

> *But when the mind rests and the dark light stills,*
> *the tree will rise untethered to its station*

— Don Paterson, "Phantom V"

Nothing will be impossible for you though nothing at all seems
possible in the murk of the mudpuddle where you are looking
for yourself, clods of earth kicked from all the earth moving past
you, its many cloven feet and buckled leather boots send tremors
through what once was water

and shakes and shivers the timbers of your soul. It was
Shakespeare who said, "Sweet are the uses of adversity," who knew
something of the soul fallen to the earth, whatever covering or
shell it had, obliterated, crushed by gravity and the hard clay which
seems made to break us but breaks

itself in season, swallows us up whole, our soft and trembling
bodies cast into the dark shafts of this cracked world where we
keep on falling until all we can recall is the downward descent
of our days, our bodies never noticed the soil, the gestation, the
summer and spring, and sprout.

Heroes

The Death of Superman was announced by Henry Cavill himself
on Instagram tonight. A former fat kid who blossomed, Superman,
well, the now-*former* Supes, didn't even put up his usual square-
jawed smile. He just said "onward and upward" on his way down.

He wouldn't hit so hard if Captain America, Chris Evans, hadn't
hung up the shield just a couple of years ago. At my age, one
should probably have fewer idols, or obsessions, but as a former
fat kid I've always been a step behind. Look, I even have these two
tattoos

willing myself, maybe, to be an Avenger or even a Man of Steel.
But who are we kidding? It's hard these days to want to get to
the gym or get up at all, or even try another app, much less put
yourself out there. What's the point? When even earth's mightiest
heroes could—

(Jack Reacher is towering, all muscle, all business, all sincerity, he,
the actor Alan Ritchson, gives his own Instagram update, shaky,
he talks about being suicidal, about suffering, he writes, "how to
suffer less" and, later, "I want us to believe… make magic again…
aspire")

never see it coming? Give me a couple of days though, a week tops,
and I'll be back at it. Belief is muscle memory that kicks in. We
were all heroes— Mariah Carey released "Hero" the fall after
high school. Mom was in the living room watching her, crying,
believing each word,

I'd just told her about enlisting, "I'm so proud of you, baby"—once.

Billy Collins Is Bored with My Dead Mother
after "The Lanyard"

The other day, as I often do, I thought of my dead mother
which is to say I lack the luxury not to think of her
like the former US Poet Laureate, Billy Collins, who found
himself famous (by poet standards) due, he might tell you
in a dozen of his own poems, to his own dead mother
who quit her job to take up reading verse to her darling.

My mother worked two jobs, had an undiagnosed breakdown,
then stopped working altogether, read me *Where the Red Fern
Grows* once, which I never forgot, how the plant grew from love
and from loss, something you will find in the L section
of the dictionary where ol' Billy Goat Collins plucked up *lanyard*
to travel back to his own dead mother, an ancient practice—

kaddish, to word your way to the past in the present, pray
yourself like the esteemed bard of the Bronx back to the lake
where he summered, or this lesser, browner, gayer, later
shadow, to the ghetto where I survived, back to mothers
long laid to rest, to say we won't forget them, or we'll try
as best we can. Except, here comes Collins in his silver years

to tell *The New York Times*, "When it comes to dead relatives,"
and I picture him when I met him, "I'm out." When two women
read their poems (one would become the new laureate), Collins
scribbled out notes for each on how they might improve, unasked.
Some people are like that. My mother once jumped on a woman
and pounded her face into the ground. I wish Billy could've met her.

El Roi
for Dad

Fathers are a mystery to their boys.
They walk ahead, troubled, mumbling to themselves,
turning around to tell us some hard truth
or some old promise or prayer:
Like sand on the shore!
Like stars in the sky!

I learned to stay back, to ask questions.
Not my brother. He woke up early and cut the wood,
tied it in a large bundle and burdened himself
all the way to the Land of Moriah.

I watched our father sharpen his blade.
No matter what you've heard, I loved my brother.
I sent the servants to follow. They said,
"Listen to him going on!"
Like sand on the shore!
Like stars in the sky!

My mother used to tell me about a desert
and her own weighted load, a child swaddled
and starving, an angel, a message to
"Fall down in wonder!"

And they were gone so long, I did
start to think of her stories, and of the old man
who eyed me like I'd suddenly burst
a spark, a conflagration.
Like sand on the shore!
Like stars in the sky!

With fear and trembling, we follow.
With flint and fuel, we flame.

Vegas, Sober
Caesars Palace, 2023

Amethyst sunset above, but Dad asked to meet
him for lunch because he cannot stay up too late.
Soon the ceiling sun recycles. Dad is going to be late.

Three girls, arms locked like a commercial or an ad
for friendship, heels and night skirts, shuffle by laughing
that offensive joy of young ignorance. Dad orders a beer

says he can't handle anything harder these days.
I remember the balloon glass of cognac, a gold and diamond
watch, my young father's avarice and cupidity. "Dad," it's who he is,

"How is your heart?" why I've braved this desert city
forever edging collapse. Like his lung. Like several marriages. He
smiles, two more beers down, for my concern or more girls passing—

Dad never answers me but asks me if I am dating.
He says it's not good to be alone. That's why he is married
again. Guys pass in shorts and caps, laughing. "Son, have a drink."

Lost in the Pacific

I never thought I'd be so tired.

— Jules, *St. Elmo's Fire*

Before I was afraid of the ocean,
I'd swim in it. No thought of the depth
or its many ways of killing me. Once
I was young and brave or foolish,
kept going away from the voices onshore
telling me to stay where it is safe, to stay

close to land
          close to home
                    close enough

until it all went silent. Out so far
the voices stop, you look around
and cannot find your way, what seemed
so clear just moments before an impulse
kept you moving in any direction
than the one you knew. When you pass

the shallow waters
          the bright buoys
                    the rope

marking where you should end,
you start to feel tired, the seascape
a cold, black unknown that goes on
forever in all directions, your panic
a ripple on the surface that dies out
before it reaches back to land. Look
up at the sun, catch your breath, listen

for the seagulls
        for the clicking pod
                of dolphins

who somehow don't terrify you
even though they are enormous, could
bat you down twenty feet below, could
be you're too tired to care, could be
it wasn't dolphins at all. But then
how did you get back? And how can you
explain what it was like out there? Why
you don't swim anymore.

You're afraid?
        You're wiser?
                You don't have to.

If I Can't

go back to the pier where stands
a statue erected sometime in my twenties
of a merchant marine taking in the Pacific –
go back, go back to an afternoon
skipping class sophomore year with Cody
on a bus to Shoreline Village, looking out –
go back, go back, go back to the ocean
where my mother's ashes were sent out –
I must make do with the view I had.

Arwen at the River

Waters

How many times have we promised ourselves, our whole selves
for a worthy sacrifice?

Here is my power and will, every last drop, may it serve this stance
or purpose or could-be love—

Listen

Where are you going, my would-be love? Can you not see all I give
for you to give back—Come back! Give back!

Where your treasure is, they say, one may find whatever keeps you
breathing, whatever brings the blood

Flow waters

Into this pale face by the water that doesn't look back, the water
that rolls ever further from your wish

Into its own kind of force fed by our own empty hands, empty
selves gallop and shake our manes of waves

Loud water

What grace is given me, let it pass, let it pass, let it pass, pass.

Oh, the Huge Manatee!

Ivy, my basset hound, sleeps on the plush manatee she got for Christmas. It's the first Christmas in a long time when I didn't buy gifts for the nieces and nephews on account of being unemployed half the year. If you're gonna lose a job, it's good to have dogs to keep you grounded, to keep you from contemplating what men my age contemplate in the face of tragedy or loss or loneliness. She rolls on her back and nuzzles her toy, her loose skin upside down, showing her teeth, makes her look like she's smiling in her sleep. What does she care about my deflated ego, pride, and bank account? Here is a warm home, a treat before bed, this giant manatee meant for a dog twice her size, and her little brother, Bucky, nearby.

Bucky has been eyeing his sister's new toy for weeks. As she drags it gently from room to room, he follows along snipping at its flat tail. Bucky is a Jack Russell terrier, bred for digging and hunting small prey. I hear Ivy snoring over a YouTube video I'm watching where two people are debating the murder of a UnitedHealthcare CEO. Murder is a terrible thing, of course, but I am sympathetic to the woman arguing that sometimes people get pushed too far. The guy she's arguing with says, "What about our humanity?" and I miss the rest. Bucky made quick work of Ivy's favorite animal, and now she's baying as if it were real. And I remember thinking of seeing my former boss get hit by a bus like in *Mean Girls*. How I'd laugh.

From the Fish

I have fears that I have failed,
like the grass, my spirit bends –
bending, failing, I get help
when I call on You again.
>In the good times and the bad,
>with the changing of a wind,
>when I'm weakest, I am glad
>I may call on You again.
Though I've conquered enemies,
and I've gathered many friends,
when they seem the same to me,
I must call on You again.

There are those who point and laugh
when I say that You're my friend;
and when I have had enough
I must call on You again.
>In the good times and the bad,
>with the changing of a wind,
>when I'm weakest, I am glad
>I may call on You again.
Like a ship, I'm tossed about
in an ocean without end;
without luxury to doubt,
I must call on You again.

Sandy Tells Me About Dead Pine Trees

"Mother didn't consider much to be trash," it's Christmas Eve, Sandy changes the subject from her husband's health, keeps a steady eye on him across the table. "People throw out useful things all the time, like Christmas trees the day after Christmas."

Robyn says there are places where you can rent a tree for the season and bring it back to the farm when you're done. They come in little pots. They get planted when they outgrow the pots. He read about them on the internet.

"But what if you kill it?" Lee, their son, ever skeptical of his father's stories, challenges this concept. "Or what if you don't want to give it back? How will they find you?"

It's past midnight. We all have to be up early in the morning to ogle Robyn and Sandy's granddaughter, the only child among us, opening her presents, looking for that rush from our past that passes too fast. We are not so much contemplating Lee's questions as we are attempting to stretch another Christmas to its limits.

Sandy guesses the tree farm would find you. Lee asks how that could be, but she moves on, "There's nothing like piling up pine trees after Christmas and jumping in them."

We all look around the table. One of us, maybe all of us ask, "Why would you do that?"

"Because it's fun," Sandy says, smiling, perhaps returning at that moment to a day after Christmas, old friends wiping tree sap on their sleeves, each one daring the others to jump first, all of their mothers still alive, unlike that pile of trees.

Robyn is getting sicker. But he married a woman who is always the first to jump.

"It doesn't sound like fun at all," Lee looks to me for agreement, "Sounds painful. It's masochism is what it is."

Sandy looks at her watch and tells Robyn he can grab the stuff in the kitchen. Ask one of us for help if he needs it. Lee keeps going on about her crazy Wichita Falls stories, the dumpster diving and the dead Christmas trees. "Why would you jump into a pile of pain?"

"Honey," she kisses her son on the cheek, puts on her coat, "That's life."

Robyn has gathered far too much from the kitchen to carry out on his own. Still, he's surveying his sons and his wife, "It was a good goddamn night!"

We laugh. We're worried. We say goodnight. We'll struggle to get up in the morning. But we will. As long as we can. Because it's fun.

Mountaintops
for the Lathams

When you make friends at a certain age, you begin with your past
self. If you don't begin there, you get there as soon as you can. You
find a way to bring whomever you were into the conversation.
I don't really know why this is. If I had to guess, I'd say it has
something to do with the self we see in the mirror in the morning
in the present. That self is better in some ways, surer, wiser, but
also cautious and wary. Not nearly as exciting nor as sexy as
you remember. That self takes another look in the mirror before
leaving the house. That self is always second-guessing. That self
misses what it used to be.

"We didn't summit," Michael corrects Lisa when I ask about the
picture of them in Nepal, "But we did make the trek." They're
smiling in front of the snow peaks, the worn prayer flags waving
behind them. There they are in India. Another of them in a midair
jump at the Chilean salt flats.

I've known Michael for over a decade, but I begin to see how much
I don't know someone I'd call one of my best friends these days.
Each little Buddha and piece of pottery, the paintings on the walls,
the bluegrass playing in the background as their sons and husky
swirl around us, reminders of what little I know. Perhaps what
little he's shared. Perhaps how little I've listened or paid attention.

Lisa is doing her best to catch me up. "We were already in our
thirties there," she smiles at me admiring their wedding photo. It's
not two decades ago but feels like a hundred.

Michael has given me the story of their prolonged romance in fits
and starts—started dating, broke up to find themselves, found
themselves back with one another, found themselves in this
picturesque neighborhood, cul-de-sac lot, two sons, good jobs, an
evening routine, a forlorn work buddy who should have met them
before all of this, back when they climbed mountains.

Not that they'd go back. Back has its blemishes. Lisa tells me about Michael's college roommate who showed up to their house on their wedding night. He decided to stay with them for the next ten or so years.

Michael fake-whispers to me about Lisa's older sister who had an affair with the cousin who is maybe coming to Christmas dinner in a couple of days. Some moments we collect by accident.

"He's not coming to Christmas," Lisa folds a giant blue three-ring binder, filled with recipes from all of the exotic places they'd been. Some moments we collect on purpose.

I can't get enough of their stories. All the imperfect players. All the twists and turns.

Our dinner is from the Mexico trip. The roast tastes like a good memory. I have a second helping.

Then it hits me: I am jealous of all of it. The way they maneuver around one another in the kitchen, the well-behaved dog, the kids too adorable to believe—the oldest one thanking me for their gift at least three or four times before we sit to eat—I am happy my friend has this. But I am also a little angry that I don't. I've lost a job I loved; I'm angry about a lot.

Dinner was about me leaving the college where Michael and I met, were hired together, taught together—English and Economics, and the students loved it, loved us. I tell Lisa I wish we'd have taken more pictures with our students. Michael agrees. Sometimes you forget to collect the moment.

Michael had invited me over for a while, but now that I'd probably be moving, the invite seemed more pressing. I'd been doing my best to keep a stiff upper lip and all of that. But here I was, unemployed and alone, and my friend and his wife are looking at these past versions of themselves so seemingly unaware of their present latitude.

"That's the current, jaded version of yourself talking," Michael says when I quip about maybe not choosing to get a doctorate again if I had a choice. Maybe not becoming a professor at all.

The comment stuns me in its honesty and truth. It's one of the most reliable things about the Michael I know: honesty and truth. I am embarrassed for my envy, for the momentary condescension of my thoughts – *They don't know how good they have it.*

Their oldest, Hays, casually comes over and says, "I really like the toy you brought us, J.D." That's thanks number six, I think.

They tell me more family stories, the mess of it all. It hasn't been easy for them. Is it easy for any of us? Even their house, this place so perfect to me at the moment, was a bit of an argument between them. It worked out, of course. As they walk me to the door to say goodnight, I see their little room of adventures. The picture of them in Nepal is positioned to be one of the first things you see when you walk in. It makes sense.

Even if you didn't reach the mountaintop, you want people to know you made the trek.

There are two ways of reading the room. One, you read yourself, you see a mirror, you see braggarts; it's like you don't know them at all. Or, two, maybe you listen a little longer, get past your own shit just long enough to see something else, something closer to true: people who know *exactly* how good they have it. People who made the effort to remind you it's not all valleys.

You suddenly wonder how many times is too many times to say, "Thank you."

When my life was ebbing away,
I remembered you, LORD

— Jonah 2:7 (NIV)

About the Author

J.D. Isip grew up in Long Beach, California, and now lives and teaches in the suburbs of Houston, Texas with his dogs, Ivy and Bucky. J.D.'s poetry, creative nonfiction, and other writings have appeared in several print and online publications, and many have been nominated for Pushcart and Best of the Net recognition. *Reluctant Prophets* is J.D.'s third full-length collection and second publication with Moon Tide Press. His other titles include *Pocketing Feathers* (Sadie Girl Press, 2015) and *Kissing the Wound* (Moon Tide Press, 2023).

Notes

"What We Deserve." Sermon referenced by Matt Chandler, February 19, 2023. Quotes and allusions to the movie, *A Few Good Men* (1992).

"These Gays Are Trying to Murder Me." Based on the second season of HBO's *The White Lotus,* specifically Episode 5 ("That's Amore") and Episode 7 ("Arrivederci").

"Frog and Toad Are Friends." Quotes in fourth stanza, attributed to Frog, are from Arnold Lobel in an interview he did with Roni Natov and Geraldine Deluca (*The Lion and the Unicorn* 1.1, 1977).

"Writing Against Oblivion." Long quotes from David Bartholomae's essay, "Inventing the University" (*Journal of Basic Writing* 5.1, 1986).

"What You Catch." Based on the HBO series and the Naughty Dog/Sony videogame, *The Last of Us,* specifically Episode 3 ("Long, Long Time").

"A Mustard Seed." Phrase about "timbers" adapted from Andrew Peterson's "The Silence of God."

Additional art:

Johannes I. Sadeler, "Jonah is thrown Overboard by Fishermen" (ca. 1582-1584)
John Collier, "Priestess of Delphi" (1891)
Giuseppe Angeli, "Elijah Taken Up in a Chariot of Fire" (ca. 1740-1755)
Peter Paul Rubens, "Daniel in the Lions' Den" (ca. 1614-1616)

Acknowledgements

Many thanks to the kind editors who first published the following poems, sometimes in slightly different forms:

"Nineveh, Again" *Fathom Magazine*
"The Lowest Part of the Ship" *Solum Journal*
"The Hard Stuff" *The Rye Whiskey Review*
"Jehovah Shammah" *Calla Press*
"Don't Tell Me" *The Blue Mountain Review*
"The Honey Remembers the Honeycomb" *Prairie Home Magazine*
"What Is Your Sign?" *Have Has Had*
"Friend of the Monster," "What You Catch,"
  "MJ & the Elephant Man" *Fevers of the Mind*
"Vanilla" *Dumpster Fire Press*
"What Used to Be McCarran Airport, Las Vegas" *Cleaver Magazine*
"Have You Ever Been So Lonely?" *The Sunshine Lounge*
"Where You Got Your Shoes,"
  "Hyperion: 800 Years a Redwood" *The Belfast Review*
"All of My Red Flags Are Heart-Shaped" *Swim Press*
"These Gays Are Trying to Murder Me" *Drip Lit: A Literary Journal*
"Another Look at Lonely" *Bear Paw Arts Journal*
"I Wasn't Finished" *Stone Circle Review*
"Before the Afterworld" *Psaltery & Lyre*
"Cope" *As It Ought To Be Magazine*
"Ode to Frito Pie" *Good River Review*
  (Nominated for *Best of the Net 2024*)
"It Won't Break My Heart to Say Goodbye" *Hobo Camp Review*
"Every Party" *Cider Press Review*
"Phantom Limbs" *Rough Diamond Poetry Journal*
"Giraffe Tattoo" *Trampoline* (Nominated for *Best of the Net 2024*)
"Arwen at the River," "El Roi," "Heroes,"
  "Frog and Toad Are Friends" *Lothlorien Poetry Journal*
"Billy Collins Is Bored with My Dead Mother"
  JAKE: The Anti-Literary Magazine
"Past the Crickets in the Tall Summer Grass"
  Scavengers Literary Magazine

"Straight for the Bear" *As You Were:*
    Military Experiences & Arts Literary Journal (M.E.A.)
"Writing Against Oblivion" *The Hooghly Review*
"Lost in the Pacific" *Otherwise Magazine,*
    also appears on the *Our California* project
"Oh, the Huge Manatee!" *Mythic Picnic*
"From the Fish" *Agape Review*
"Sandy Tells Me About Dead Pine Trees"
    Well Read (Nominated for *Pushcart Prize* 2024)
"Mountaintops" *Superstition Review*
"The Real Thing," "Owner of a Lonely Heart" *Blue Daisies*

An early version of this collection was a Semi-Finalist 2023
Richard Snyder Memorial Book Prize.

Thanks

I've written often about suicidal ideation. I open this collection with the words of Jim May's terrific "Sentimental Hogwash" which deals with his own struggles. Unfortunately, we are not unique. I have lost far too many friends and colleagues to suicide, and I have seen the heartbreak and destruction of those left in the aftermath. Kindness isn't a cure, but it sure as hell helps. It is cliché but true that *I would not be here today* without the love and support, and kindness of my family, friends, and colleagues. And without words like those from Jim's poem, from a movie like *All Over the Guy*, from a play like *The Seagull*, or from a song like Rich Mullins' "Elijah," each offering, in their own way, "a light to you in dark places" as Galadriel would say.

I am indebted to Eric Morago, Ellen Webre, HanaLena Fennel, and everyone at Moon Tide Press for their faith in my work and continual support. Likewise, I am humbled to call so many in the poetry community friends including Cynthia Atkins, Anders Carlson-Wee, Richie Hofmann, and Denton Loving who all offered such kind words about this collection. I am grateful to my dear friends Lynne Kemen and Bright Hill Press, Nicole Tallman and ELJ Editions "Be Well" Reading Series, Charles K. Carter and his Sunday Sweet Chats, Ben Trigg and The Ugly Mug, Sarah Howser Northam, Jacob Pichnarcik, and Marilyn Harris Lewis at East Texas A&M University (formerly A&M-Commerce), and many, many others for offering me a place to read my work and commune with like-minds. I am also grateful to my friend, Clifford Brooks, for the opportunity to read work and do interviews for *The Blue Mountain Review*.

My mentors continue to echo in everything I write. Thank you to Donna Dunbar-Odom, Karen Roggenkamp, Susan Stewart, Christopher Gonzalez (the *other* "big scary brown guy"), and Hunter Hayes at East Texas A&M; Cornel Bonca, Marty Blaine, J. Chris Westgate, Kay Stanton, and my dear friend, Irena Praitis, at Cal State Fullerton; from Long Beach City College, Laura Scavuzzo Wheeler, Frank X. Gaspar, Tony Gargano, and the late poet Stephen Perry who stopped me after our last workshop of the semester some 30 years ago and said, "I don't say this to every student. J.D., I want you to know you've got *it*. Keep writing." Advice I, of course, ignored for almost twenty years; I am trying to make up for lost time (aren't we all?). The kids at David Starr Jordan High School who knew anything about writing owed it all to a singular figure, the fierce and big-hearted Marie Tollstrup.

They say you can measure a man by the friends he keeps, and it has always been my goal in life to *keep* as many as possible. Love to my childhood muses, Cody, Carrie, Laura, Shonna, Shannan, Josh, Rose, Manny, and Lalo; those who populated my stunted adulthood in the Air Force, Rob, Brian, Shane, Tim, Trish, and Hill; my Disney family including Marty, Dave, Michael, Dean, Jolene, Christy, Vanessa, Richelle, Paula, Lissette, Diane, Mary, and John; my CSUF grad school cohort who would solve the problems of the world out in the parking lot, Vanessa, Katie, Berlyn, Bruce, Sariah, Joe, Jeff, and my "little sister" Kristen; the bright minds and big hearts in Commerce including, Mary, Alyse (and Edmund), JJ, Brandon, Toni, Randi, Allyson, Erin, and Omer; and many, many others at each of these places and at my former places of employment.

Speaking of, I thank Wharton County Junior College for their support. Especially TK, Patrick, Hector, Joshua (and Jessica), Wendy, and Vicki who keeps us all sane.

Since this is getting entirely too long and I cannot hope to name everyone, let me wrap up with a special thank you and deep love for the players on the stage of this current production: my fabulous and dear friends, Khimen, Randy, and "the kids," and Anne and Jack; Kelly Andrews, Deb Hall, and Rachel Walker; my brothers Sean and the Ferrier Watsons, Vince (and the new Liberato family), W. Scott Cheney (and his ever-expanding brood), J. Michael and the Lathams, Mark (and the Krogstads), Tony Howard and R. Scott Yarbrough.

Finally, my family: my moral guideposts, Yvonne and Jeff Flynn and Joe and Magen Isip; my brothers Sam and Chris; Rosa Meredith; my little sisters, Jeannette, Joannah, and Jackie (who continue to astonish me with their grace and goodness); all of my nieces and nephews; and my father, who has lived a damn good life (and is probably on a cruise right now). Of course, my mother, Margie, and my big brother, Bill, will live on in anything I write. I could not love you more.

I thank God for this life, and I thank, you, reader, for dropping in for a bit.

Also Available from Moon Tide Press

Enormous Blue Umbrella, Donna Hilbert (2025)
Sky Leaning Toward Winter, Terri Niccum (2024)
Living the Sundown: A Caregiving Memoir, G. Murray Thomas (2024)
Figure Study, Kathryn de Lancellotti (2024)
Suffer for This: Love, Sex, Marriage, & Rock 'N' Roll,
    Victor D. Infante (2024)
What Blooms in the Dark, Emily J. Mundy (2024)
Fable, Bryn Wickerd (2024)
Diamond Bars 2, David A. Romero (2024)
Safe Handling, Rebecca Evans (2024)
More Jerkumstances: New & Selected Poems, Barbara Eknoian (2024)
Dissection Day, Ally McGregor (2023)
He's a Color Until He's Not, Christian Hanz Lozada (2023)
The Language of Fractions, Nicelle Davis (2023)
Paradise Anonymous, Oriana Ivy (2023)
Now You Are a Missing Person, Susan Hayden (2023)
Maze Mouth, Brian Sonia-Wallace (2023)
Tangled by Blood, Rebecca Evans (2023)
Another Way of Loving Death, Jeremy Ra (2023)
Kissing the Wound, J.D. Isip (2023)
Feed It to the River, Terhi K. Cherry (2022)
Beat Not Beat: An Anthology of California Poets
    Screwing on the Beat and Post-Beat Tradition (2022)
When There Are Nine: Poems Celebrating the
    Life and Achievements of Ruth Bader Ginsburg (2022)
The Knife Thrower's Daughter, Terri Niccum (2022)
2 Revere Place, Aruni Wijesinghe (2022)
Here Go the Knives, Kelsey Bryan-Zwick (2022)
Trumpets in the Sky, Jerry Garcia (2022)
Threnody, Donna Hilbert (2022)
A Burning Lake of Paper Suns, Ellen Webre (2021)
Instructions for an Animal Body, Kelly Gray (2021)
Head *V* Heart: New & Selected Poems, Rob Sturma (2021)
Sh!t Men Say to Me: A Poetry Anthology
    in Response to Toxic Masculinity (2021)
Flower Grand First, Gustavo Hernandez (2021)

Everything is Radiant Between the Hates, Rich Ferguson (2020)
When the Pain Starts: Poetry as Sequential Art,
        Alan Passman (2020)
This Place Could Be Haunted If I Didn't Believe in Love,
        Lincoln McElwee (2020)
Impossible Thirst, Kathryn de Lancellotti (2020)
Lullabies for End Times, Jennifer Bradpiece (2020)
Crabgrass World, Robin Axworthy (2020)
Contortionist Tongue, Dania Ayah Alkhouli (2020)
The only thing that makes sense is to grow, Scott Ferry (2020)
Dead Letter Box, Terri Niccum (2019)
Tea and Subtitles: Selected Poems 1999-2019, Michael Miller (2019)
At the Table of the Unknown, Alexandra Umlas (2019)
The Book of Rabbits, Vince Trimboli (2019)
Everything I Write Is a Love Song to the World,
        David McIntire (2019)
Letters to the Leader, HanaLena Fennel (2019)
Darwin's Garden, Lee Rossi (2019)
Dark Ink: A Poetry Anthology Inspired by Horror (2018)
Drop and Dazzle, Peggy Dobreer (2018)
Junkie Wife, Alexis Rhone Fancher (2018)
The Moon, My Lover, My Mother, & the Dog,
        Daniel McGinn (2018)
Lullaby of Teeth: An Anthology of Southern California Poetry (2017)
Angels in Seven, Michael Miller (2016)
A Likely Story, Robbi Nester (2014)
Embers on the Stairs, Ruth Bavetta (2014)
The Green of Sunset, John Brantingham (2013)
The Savagery of Bone, Timothy Matthew Perez (2013)
The Silence of Doorways, Sharon Venezio (2013)
Cosmos: An Anthology of Southern California Poetry (2012)
Straws and Shadows, Irena Praitis (2012)
In the Lake of Your Bones, Peggy Dobreer (2012)
I Was Building Up to Something, Susan Davis (2011)
Hopeless Cases, Michael Kramer (2011)
One World, Gail Newman (2011)
What We Ache For, Eric Morago (2010)
Now and Then, Lee Mallory (2009)
Pop Art: An Anthology of Southern California Poetry (2009)

In the Heaven of Never Before, Carine Topal (2008)
A Wild Region, Kate Buckley (2008)
Carving in Bone: An Anthology of Orange County Poetry (2007)
Kindness from a Dark God, Ben Trigg (2007)
A Thin Strand of Lights, Ricki Mandeville (2006)
Sleepyhead Assassins, Mindy Nettifee (2006)
Tide Pools: An Anthology of Orange County Poetry (2006)
Lost American Nights: Lyrics & Poems, Michael Ubaldini (2006)

Patrons

Moon Tide Press would like to thank the following people for their support in helping publish the finest poetry from the Southern California region. To sign up as a patron, visit www.moontidepress.com or send an email to publisher@moontidepress.com.

Anonymous
Robin Axworthy
Conner Brenner
Nicole Connolly
Bill Cushing
Susan Davis
Kristen Baum DeBeasi
Peggy Dobreer
Kate Gale
Dennis Gowans
Alexis Rhone Fancher
HanaLena Fennel
Half Off Books & Brad T. Cox
Donna Hilbert
Jim & Vicky Hoggatt
Michael Kramer
Ron Koertge & Bianca Richards
Gary Jacobelly
Ray & Christi Lacoste
Jeffery Lewis
Zachary & Tammy Locklin
Lincoln McElwee
David McIntire
José Enrique Medina

Michael Miller &
Rachanee Srisavasdi
Michelle & Robert Miller
Ronny & Richard Morago
Terri Niccum
Andrew November
Jeremy Ra
Luke & Mia Salazar
Jennifer Smith
Roger Sponder
Andrew Turner
Rex Wilder
Mariano Zaro
Wes Bryan Zwick

www.ingramcontent.com/pod-product-compliance
Lightning Source LLC
Chambersburg PA
CBHW031140090426
42738CB00008B/1169